SETTING THE RECORD STRAIGHT
JOSEPH SMITH
PROPHET

Cover: The illustrations on the cover represent Joseph Smith in two settings. The kneeling figure represents young Joseph praying to God to know which church he should join. The standing figure depicts the more mature Joseph sharing gospel truths.

SETTING THE RECORD STRAIGHT

JOSEPH SMITH
THE MORMON PROPHET

Susan Easton Black

Millennial Press, Inc.
P.O. Box 1741
Orem, UT 84059

ISBN: 1-932597-38-7

Cover design and typesetting by Adam Riggs

Dedication

To my grandson Bryce Easton for believing Joseph Smith was a prophet of God.

Contents

Acknowledgments

Providing answers to the questions asked in this text would not have been possible without access to significant resources in archives and libraries. I am very appreciative of the staff at the Church History Library in Salt Lake City and the staff at the L. Tom Perry Special Collections at Brigham Young University for their kind assistance. The same courteous assistance was given by research assistant Jennifer Heyman Ray, editor Heather Seferovich, and colleagues at BYU. To each of them, I express gratitude and admiration for their many talents.

Introduction

Prominent journalists are too often misinformed about Joseph Smith, the founder of the Church of Jesus Christ of Latter-day Saints. On any given day, television, print media, and the Internet carry stories about him filled with fragmented truths or altogether incorrect information. While some of these problems can stem from ignorance, in other cases journalists understand that intelligent, thoughtful stories don't get much notice. In an era saturated with media, it's hard to attract a reader's attention without using sensationalism.

For more than a century and a half, Joseph Smith has received a disproportionate amount of ridicule in the media. From his youthful days in Palmyra, New York, to his martyrdom in Carthage, Illinois, to the faith he founded that is headquartered in Salt Lake City, Utah, there have always been those who find his claims strange and his doctrine threatening. Despite accusations, physical attacks, and judicial harassment, Joseph Smith always affirmed that he had been called by God to be a prophet, "I could not deny it, neither dared I do it; at least I knew that by so doing I would offend God, and come under condemnation."[1]

What was it about Joseph Smith that led others to ridicule him? Reverend Diedrich Willer of Fayette, New York, wrote, "The greatest imposter of our times in the field of religion is no doubt a certain Joseph Smith. This new sect [that he started known as Mormonism] should not cause the Christian Church great astonishment." Willer went on to explain that off-shoots like Mormonism "have all been absorbed in the Sea of the Past and marked with the stamp of oblivion. This will also be the lot of the Mormonites, and, I hope, while it is still in the bud."[2] If Willer were still alive, he would be dismayed that the religion Joseph Smith started is still functioning in the twenty-first century and that it claims over thirteen million members located throughout the world.

Though people like Willer dismissed Joseph Smith and inaccurately predicted his church would fail, many more examined the young prophet's claims and joined the new faith. Joseph Smith announced, "Many opened their houses to us. Our meetings were well attended, and many began to pray fervently to Almighty God, that He would give them wisdom to understand the truth."[3] Readers will learn that truth became a watch cry for Joseph Smith and his followers.

Are Latter-day Saints, commonly called Mormons, deceived or are the claims of Joseph Smith and the Church of Jesus Christ of Latter-day Saints valid? What follows is an examination of his life and beliefs along with what contemporaries thought of him. Readers can examine the evidence presented here and decide for themselves what they think of Joseph Smith, the Mormon Prophet.

Joseph Smith's Life in Historical Context

1805

October 21 — Royal British Navy fleet, commanded by Horatio Nelson, defeats French and Spanish fleets at Battle of Trafalgar. Napoleon's threatened invasion of Britain ends.

November 7 — Merriwether Lewis and William Clark expedition reaches Pacific Ocean via the Columbia River.

December 23 — Joseph Smith Jr., son of Joseph Smith Sr. and Lucy Mack, is born in Sharon Township, Windsor County, Vermont.

1812

June 18 — U.S. President James Madison signs the declaration commencing the War of 1812 with Great Britain.

1813

Joseph contracts typhus fever; complications require a leg operation by Dr. Nathan Smith, et. al., West Lebanon, New Hampshire.

Smith family rents the Constant Murdock farm, Norwich, Vermont.

Englishman William Horrocks produces first power loom.

Pride and Prejudice by Jane Austen and *The Swiss Family Robinson* by Johann Rudolf Wyss are published.

September 7   The term "Uncle Sam" is first used to mean the United States, *Troy (New York) Post*.

1814

August   Washington, D.C. is sacked and burned by British forces.

1816

Smiths move from Norwich, Vermont, to the village of Palmyra, New York.

Gioacchino Antonio Rossinni's opera "The Barber of Seville" is performed at Rome's Teatro Argentina.

December   James Monroe becomes president of United States.

1820

Ancient Greek sculpture "Venus de Milo" discovered on Greek island.

March 6   Missouri Compromise, admitting Missouri as a slave state, passes U.S. Congress.

Early Spring   Joseph receives First Vision, Palmyra.

April 7   Spanish Inquisition, begun in 1478, ends.

1823

September 21-22	Joseph has interviews with angel Moroni; sees gold plates at Hill Cumorah.
November 19	Joseph's brother Alvin Smith dies.
December 2	President James Monroe announces "Monroe Doctrine," excluding European intervention in politics of American republics.

1825

October-November	Josiah Stowell hires Joseph to dig for Spanish treasure in Harmony, Pennsylvania; Joseph meets Emma Hale.
October 26	Erie Canal opens between Lake Erie at Buffalo and the Hudson River.

1826

March 20	Joseph is tried and acquitted of disorderly conduct, South Bainbridge, New York.

1827

	Frenchman Benoit Fourneyron devises water-wheel turbine.
	Sailing vessel embarks from New Orleans, Louisiana, and arrives in Liverpool, England, in twenty-six days.
January 18	Joseph and Emma are married by Zachariah Tarble, South Bainbridge.
September 22	Joseph obtains the Book of Mormon plates from the angel Moroni at Hill Cumorah.

1828

Andrew Jackson becomes president of United States.

February
Martin Harris shows Book of Mormon characters to Charles Anthon and Samuel L. Mitchill.

June-July
While in the possession of Martin Harris, 116 manuscript pages of the Book of Lehi are lost (D&C 3, 10).

July 4
Groundbreaking ceremonies mark beginning of first U.S. passenger railroad, the Baltimore & Ohio.

1829

U.S. Prison Discipline Society claims 75,000 Americans are imprisoned each year for debt. Half of the debtors owe less than $20.

Frenchman Bathelemy Thimonnier develops the first practical sewing machine.

April 7
Joseph resumes translation of ancient record with scribe Oliver Cowdery.

May 15
Joseph and Oliver receive Aaronic Priesthood from John the Baptist, near the Susquehanna River (D&C 13).

May-June
Joseph and Oliver receive Melchizedek Priesthood and Apostleship from Peter, James, and John near the Susquehanna River.

June 11
Joseph secures the copyright for the Book of Mormon.

June	The Three and the Eight Witnesses view the gold plates.
June	Joseph completes the Book of Mormon translation, Fayette, New York.
August	Book of Mormon printing begins at E. B. Grandin's print shop, Palmyra.

1830

William Sublette and Jedediah Strong lead first wagon train to the Rocky Mountains.

March 26	Book of Mormon goes on sale at E. B. Grandin's Bookstore, Palmyra.
April 6	The Church of Christ (later known as the Church of Jesus Christ of Latter-day Saints) organized at Whitmer farm, Fayette (D&C 20-22).
May 28	U.S. President Andrew Jackson signs Indian Removal Act providing for the general removal of Indians to lands west of the Mississippi River.
June	Joseph receives the revelation known as Moses, chapter one, Harmony.
June 9	First conference of the Church is held, Fayette.
September-October	Four missionaries are called to visit the Lamanites (Indians) (D&C 28, 30, 32).
December	Sidney Rigdon serves as scribe for the New Translation of the Bible (D&C 35).

1831

Virginia farmer Cyrus Hall McCormick demonstrates McCormick Reaper, which allows one person to do the work of five.

January 2	Joseph receives revelations to gather followers to Ohio (D&C 37-38).
February 1	Joseph arrives in Kirtland, Ohio.
February 9	Joseph receives the law of the Church and the consecration of properties (D&C 42).
June 3	First high priests are ordained at a Church conference, Kirtland.
July 20	Joseph designates Independence, Missouri, as the center place of Zion (D&C 57).
August 3	Joseph dedicates the temple site in Independence.
December 12	Republican Party holds the first nominating convention of a U.S. major party.

1832

January 25	Church members sustain Joseph as president of the High Priesthood, Amherst, Ohio.
February 16	Joseph and Sidney Rigdon receive a vision of the three degrees of glory (D&C 76).
March 24	A mob tars and feathers Joseph near the John Johnson farmhouse, Hiram, Ohio.
May 21	U.S. Democratic Party formally adopts present name at political convention, Baltimore, Maryland.
June	The Church newspaper, *The Evening and the Morning Star* is published, Independence.
December 25	Joseph receives a revelation known as the "Prophecy on War" (D&C 87).
December 27-28	Joseph receives a revelation known as the "Olive Leaf," commanding that a temple be built in

Kirtland and a School of the Prophets be organized (D&C 88).

1833

Oxford University vicar John Henry Newman writes verses to hymn, "Lead Kindly Light."

January 22-23 School of the Prophets commences, Kirtland.

February 27 Joseph receives a revelation known as the "Word of Wisdom" (D&C 89).

March 18 First Presidency organized.

July 23 Kirtland Temple cornerstones are laid.

December 18 Joseph Smith Sr. becomes patriarch to the Church.

1834

Frenchman Louis Braille devises Braille system.

February 17 First stake and high council of the Church is organized, Kirtland.

May 5 Joseph leaves Kirtland as the leader of Zion's Camp.

October 16 London's Houses of Parliament are destroyed by fire.

1835

United States has 1,098 miles of railroad operating.

February 14 Joseph organizes the Quorum of the Twelve Apostles.

February 28 Joseph organizes the Quorum of the Seventy.

March 28	Joseph receives a revelation on the priesthood (D&C 107).
July 6	Joseph purchases Egyptian mummies and papyri from Michael Chandler.
August 17	The Church adopts the Doctrine and Covenants as scripture, Kirtland.
December 16	New York City loses 674 structures to fire.

1836

	Martin Van Buren becomes president of United States.
	75 percent of employed Americans engage in agriculture.
January 21	Joseph receives spiritual manifestations in the Kirtland Temple (D&C 137).
March 6	The Alamo falls, San Antonio, Texas; U.S. war with Mexico ensues.
March 27	Joseph dedicates the Kirtland Temple (D&C 109).
April 3	Joseph and Oliver Cowdery receive a series of visions in the Kirtland Temple—Christ, Moses, Elias and Elijah appear (D&C 110).

1837

March	A U.S. economic depression begins after the failure of cotton brokerage Herman Briggs & Co.
March	Kirtland Safety Society Anti-Bank fails.
June	First seven Latter-day Saint missionaries leave for England; they arrive July 19, 1837.
June 20	Queen Victoria begins a sixty-four-year reign over the British Empire.

1838

Charles Dickens publishes *Oliver Twist*.

Famine kills thousands in northern Ireland.

January 12	Joseph leaves Kirtland to escape mob violence.
March 14	Headquarters of the Church is established in Far West, Missouri.
April 23	First transatlantic steamship service begins.
April 26	Joseph receives a revelation on the name of the Church—The Church of Jesus Christ of Latter-day Saints (D&C 115).
May 19	Joseph selects the site of Adam-ondi-Ahman, Missouri.
July 4	Church leaders lay the cornerstones for the Far West Temple.
July 8	Joseph receives a revelation on tithing (D&C 119).
August 6	Latter-day Saints suffer in election-day violence, Gallatin, Missouri.
October 27	Missouri Governor Lilburn W. Boggs issues the "extermination order."
October 30	Mob attacks Latter-day Saints at Haun's Mill, Missouri.
October 31	Joseph is taken prisoner by a Missouri militia, near Far West.
November 1	Joseph is sentenced to death by irregular courts martial; Alexander Doniphan refuses to carry out the execution order.
November 12-29	Joseph is subjected to a court of inquiry, Richmond, Missouri; he rebukes abusive guards.

December 1	Joseph is imprisoned in Liberty Jail, Liberty, Missouri.

1839

Scotsman Kirkpatrick MacMillan invents the first modern bicycle.

Chemist Christian F. Shonbein discovers the ozone layer.

Telegraph pioneer Samuel F. B. Morse makes the first daguerreotype portraits in America.

March 20-25	Joseph writes epistle from Liberty Jail to Latter-day Saints in Quincy, Illinois (D&C 121-123).
April 16	En route to trial at Columbia, Missouri, (after obtaining change of venue) Joseph escapes.
April 22	Joseph joins his family in Quincy.
May 10	Joseph moves to Commerce (later known as Nauvoo), Illinois.
October 22-March 4, 1840	Joseph travels to Washington, D.C. to petition government officials for redress of Missouri losses; meets with President Martin VanBuren.

1840

January 19	The Charles Wilkes expedition claims part of Antarctica for the United States.
March 4	Redress of Missouri losses; meets with President Martin Van Buren.
May 1	The first adhesive postage stamps sell in Britain.
August 15	Joseph introduces the ordinance of baptism for the dead.

October 5	Joseph's scribe Robert B. Thompson delivers "Treatise on Priesthood."

1841

Publisher Horace Greeley launches the *New York Tribune.*

January 19	Joseph receives a revelation to build the Nauvoo Temple and the Nauvoo House (D&C 124).
February 1	Joseph is elected to the Nauvoo City Council.
February 4	Joseph is elected as lieutenant general of the Nauvoo Legion.
April 4	U.S. President William Henry Harrison dies one month after taking office; John Tyler succeeds him.
April 6	Church leaders lay the Nauvoo Temple cornerstones.
June 4	Joseph is arrested on Missouri charges; court dismisses a writ for arrest on June 10, 1841.
August 7	Joseph's brother Don Carlos Smith dies.
November 8	Joseph dedicates the baptismal font at the Nauvoo Temple site.

1842

U.S. Congress authorizes John C. Fremont to identify a northern route to Oregon.

Massachusetts Legislature enacts a law limiting work hours of children under age twelve to ten hours per day.

January 5	Joseph begins operating the Nauvoo mercantile store (known as the Red Brick Store).

March 1	Joseph commences publishing the Book of Abraham in the *Times and Seasons*, Nauvoo.
March 17	Joseph organizes the Female Relief Society of Nauvoo with Emma Smith as president.
May 4	Joseph administers the first full temple endowments in the upper room of the Red Brick Store, Nauvoo.
May 19	Joseph becomes mayor of Nauvoo.
August 6	Joseph prophesies Latter-day Saints will be driven to the Rocky Mountains.

1843

Yellow fever kills thirteen-thousand people in the Mississippi River Valley.

Charles Dickens publishes *A Christmas Carol*.

Charles Thurber of Massachusetts pioneers the typewriter.

Skiing as a sport begins in Tromso, Norway.

July 12	Joseph records a revelation on the new and everlasting covenant of marriage (D&C 132).
August 31	Joseph moves his family into the Mansion House, Nauvoo.

1844

Karl Marx writes, "Introduction to a Critique of the Hegelian Philosophy of the Right" and declares, "Religion is the sign of the oppressed creature ... It is the opium of the people."

January 29	Joseph becomes a candidate for U.S. president.

March	Joseph gives responsibility for the Kingdom to the Twelve Apostles.
April 7	Joseph delivers the "King Follett" discourse.
May 24	Samuel Morse transmits over telegraph wire, "What hath God wrought?" from Washington, D.C., to Baltimore, Maryland.
June 7	*Nauvoo Expositor* incites anger by vilifying Joseph and calling for the repeal of the Nauvoo charter.
June 10	Nauvoo City Council declares *Nauvoo Expositor* a public nuisance.
June 27	Mob kills Joseph and his brother Hyrum, Carthage, Illinois.
June 29	Joseph is buried, Nauvoo.
July 30	Joseph's brother Samuel Harrison Smith dies.
August 8	Church members sustain Brigham Young and the Quorum of the Twelve Apostles to lead the Church.

Life of Joseph Smith

When Joseph Smith was born, did family members or near neighbors recognize him as a prophet like Moses?

Joseph Smith was born December 23, 1805, in the rural setting of Sharon, Windsor County, Vermont. Doctor Joseph A. Dennison, a country practitioner, reportedly assisted in his delivery. Years later the doctor wrote in his account book, "If I had known how he was going to turn out I'd have smothered the little cuss."[4] From the writings of Lucy Mack Smith, Joseph's mother, it is clear that she did not anticipate the prophetic calling of her newborn infant. "In the meantime we had a son," she recorded, "whom we called Joseph, after the name of his father."[5] The infant was not recognized by the attending physician or his mother as being any different from other sons born to impoverished parents in the woodlands of America.

Did the poverty of the Smith family mar Joseph Smith's childhood?

Relentless poverty stalked the Smith family in Sharon, Vermont. Subsequent moves from Sharon did not measurably improve their economic situation. Joseph's father was a farmer on rented land. In the winter, he worked as a schoolteacher to help make ends meet. When Joseph was six years old, financial circumstances of the family improved, but not for long.[6]

What compromised the health of Joseph Smith in his youth?

In 1811 a typhus fever epidemic, which left nearly six thousand dead in the Connecticut Valley, raged through the small community of Lebanon, afflicting children in the Smith household. Each child recovered from the illness without undue complications except young Joseph, who suffered from a fever for two weeks, but from side effects much longer. "Oh, father! the pain is so severe," cried Joseph. "How can I bear it!" Bear it he must for the disease settled in his "left leg & ankle & terminated in a fever sore of the worst kind." Medical practitioners, with varying degrees of expertise, proposed amputation of his foot. The mere suggestion "was like a thunderbolt to me," Mother Smith said.[7] "Young as I was, I utterly refused to give my assent to the operation," said Joseph. However, he "consented to [the doctors] Trying an experiment by removing a large portion of the bone from my left leg."[8] Surgeons operated "by boring into the bone of his leg, first on one side of the bone where it was affected, then on the other side, after which they broke it off with a pair of forceps or pincers. They thus took away large pieces of the bone."[9] Joseph's recovery was slow and painful. "Fourteen additional pieces of bone afterwards worked out before my leg healed," said Joseph.[10] Until his wounds healed, a bed and crutches were his common lot.

What caused the Smith family to leave Vermont and settle in New York?

Seeking economic freedom, the Smiths moved from Lebanon to Norwich, Vermont. In Norwich, the family worked on a rented farm, but without credit to tide them over until the first harvest. Adding to their difficulties, "The first year our crops failed; . . . The crops the second year were as the year before—a perfect failure. Mr. Smith now determined to plant once more, and if he should meet with no better success than he had the two preceding years, he would then go to the state of New York, where wheat was raised in abundance. The next year an untimely frost destroyed the crops, . . . it almost caused a famine. This was enough," wrote Mother Smith, "my husband was now altogether decided upon going to New York."[11]

Did the family go together to western New York or did Father Smith make the journey alone?

In 1816, Joseph Smith's father left the Connecticut River Valley and settled in Palmyra, New York. The family, including young Joseph, remained in Norwich for a short time until Caleb Howard, a man hired to convey Mother Smith and her eight children three hundred miles to Palmyra, was ready to begin the journey. On the journey, Howard proved "an unprincipled and unfeeling wretch, by the way in which he handled both our goods and money, as well as by his treatment of my children, especially Joseph," wrote Mother Smith. "[Howard] would compel [Joseph] to travel miles at a time on foot, notwithstanding he was still lame."[12] Joseph recalled that Howard "drove me from the wagon & made me travel in my weak state through the snow, 40 miles per day for several days, during which time I suffered the most excruciating weariness & pain." When Joseph's brothers confronted "Mr. Howard, for his treatment to me, he would knock them down with the butt of his whip." Adding to Joseph's difficulties was the driver of a passing sleigh, who deliberately knocked him to the ground. "[I was] left to wallow in my blood," wrote Joseph. It was not "until a stranger came along," that the young boy was rescued. Joseph recalled, "[The stranger] picked me up, & carried me to the Town of Palmyra."[13]

How did the Smiths support themselves in Palmyra?

Although the Smiths were "much reduced—not from indolence, but on account of many reverses of fortune, with which our lives had been rather singularly marked," wrote Mother Smith, the family redoubled its efforts with renewed courage to gain financial stability.[14] Father Smith opened a small shop on Main Street and sold gingerbread, pies, boiled eggs, and root beer to paying customers. Mother Smith painted oil-cloth coverings for tables that were sold to admiring neighbors. Family members also made and sold split-wood chairs, brooms, and baskets. Sons worked as common laborers gardening, harvesting, rocking up wells—and any other odd job that paid cash. Joseph's brother William recalled, "Whenever the neighbors wanted a good day's work done they knew where they could get a good hand."[15]

Did the Smiths purchase a farm in the village of Palmyra or did they continue to rent farmland?

For a year and a half, the Smith family worked and saved for a down payment on a hundred-acre farm. In 1818, Father Smith contracted for a farm and began making payments on acreage he hoped to own one day. The Smith farm was nestled in a wooded tract about two miles south of the Palmyra village on Stafford Road. Within the first year of their residency on that farm, "We made nearly all of the first payment, erected a log house, and commenced clearing. I believe something like thirty acres of land were got ready for cultivation the first year," wrote Mother Smith. By the second year she added, "We had a snug log house, neatly furnished, and the means of living comfortably."[16] By "the strictest kind of economy and labor," the Smith family turned heavily wooded acreage into a productive farm "admired for its good order and industry."[17]

Were the Smiths accepted socially in the Palmyra community?

With productivity and apparent permanency in the community came a sense of belonging and neighborly cordiality. "The hand of friendship was extended on every side," wrote Mother Smith. She believed, "If we might judge by external manifestations, we had every reason to believe that we had many good and affectionate friends for never have I seen more kindness or attention shown to any person or family than we received from those around us."[18]

However, cordiality extended by neighbors and new-found friends ended abruptly in 1820. The dramatic change began when fourteen-year-old Joseph Smith announced to an itinerant minister that he had seen a heavenly vision. The minister treated his announcement lightly, as if it were a figment of the boy's imagination, yet took occasion to tell others. Grown men scoffed at the idea of heavenly beings appearing in the Palmyra woods. But the unwavering affirmation of the teenager soon rancored both minister and farmer alike. Although they espoused religious leanings and even claimed heavenly raptures, it was the nature of the boy's vision that disturbed them. A divine assurance of forgiveness and a promise of grace would have been encouraged in young Joseph, not a vision of God the Father and Jesus Christ.[19] Men of the cloth preached salvation, justice, and grace—not restoration.

What was Joseph Smith's First Vision?

Joseph wrote of going into the woods on his family farm to ask God which church he should join:

> "I kneeled down and began to offer up the desires of my heart to God. I had scarcely done so, when immediately I was seized upon by some power which entirely overcame me, and had such an

astonishing influence over me as to bind my tongue so that I could not speak. Thick darkness gathered around me, and it seemed to me for a time as if I were doomed to sudden destruction. But, exerting all my powers to call upon God to deliver me out of the power of this enemy which had seized upon me, and at the very moment when I was ready to sink into despair and abandon myself to destruction—not to an imaginary ruin, but to the power of some actual being from the unseen world, who had such marvelous power as I had never before felt in any being—just at this moment of great alarm, I saw a pillar of light exactly over my head, above the brightness of the sun, which descended gradually until it fell upon me. It no sooner appeared than I found myself delivered from the enemy which held me bound. When the light rested upon me I saw two Personages, whose brightness and glory defy all description, standing above me in the air. One of them spake unto me, calling me by name and said, pointing to the other—This is My Beloved Son. Hear Him!"[20]

Was Joseph Smith mocked and persecuted for believing his vision was from God?

"Though I was an obscure boy, only between fourteen and fifteen years of age, and my circumstances in life such as to make a boy of no consequence in the world," Joseph mused, "yet men of high standing would take notice sufficient to excite the public mind against me, and create a bitter persecution."[21] For Joseph and his family, this persecution caused great alarm. Former friends suggested "not one of the male members of the Smith family were entitled to any credit whatsoever." Joseph and his father were labeled as "entirely destitute of moral character and addicted to vicious habits."[22] William Smith wrote, "We never knew we were bad folks until Joseph told his vision."[23]

After he had his First Vision, did Joseph Smith act like a prophet of God—like ancient prophets of the Old Testament?

Joseph "frequently fell into many foolish errors, and displayed the weakness of youth, and the foibles of human nature."[24] What he had observed as a contradicting message from the preachers in Palmyra was mirrored in his own youthful demeanor. However, he confessed, "I have not, neither can it be sustained, in truth, been guilty of wronging or injuring any man or society of men."[25] Yet for a boy who had seen God the Father and Jesus Christ and had suffered "severe persecution at the hands of all classes of men, both religious and irreligious, because I continued to affirm that I had seen a vision," his foolish actions caused him to feel "condemned for my weakness and imperfections."[26]

Did young Joseph Smith claim to see angels, too?

On the evening of September 21, 1823, as he pled "for forgiveness of all my sins and follies, and also for a manifestation to me, that I might know of my state and standing before him," Joseph "discovered a light appearing in my room, which continued to increase until the room was lighter than at noonday, when immediately a personage appeared at my bedside, standing in the air, for his feet did not touch the floor." As Joseph later related, the angelic personage "called me by name, and said unto me that he was a messenger sent from the presence of God to me, and that his name was Moroni."[27]

Was it from the angel that Joseph Smith learned about gold plates and early inhabitants of America?

On Sunday evening, September 21, 1823, the angel told Joseph that "God had a work for me to do; and that my name should be had for good and evil among all nations, kindreds, and tongues, or that it should be both good and evil spoken of among all people." This prophesied-conflicting reputation centered around a book written upon gold plates, and a Urim and Thummim prepared "for the purpose of translating the book." As the angel conversed with the boy, "the place where the plates were deposited" was shown him in vision—a hill just a few miles from his home. Joseph went directly to the hill he had seen in vision—'a hill of considerable size, and the most elevated of any in the neighborhood"—and there "under a stone of considerable size, lay the plates, deposited in a stone box." His attempt to take the contents of the box was forbidden by the angel. Joseph was told that "the time for bringing them forth had not yet arrived."[28]

Did the Smiths believe that young Joseph Smith had conversed with an angel sent from God?

His family accepted Joseph's description of "the ancient inhabitants of this continent, their dress, mode of traveling, and the animals upon which they rode, their cities, their buildings, with every particular; their mode of warfare; and also their religious worship. This he would do with as much ease, seemingly, as if he had spent his whole life with them," wrote his mother. "I presume our family presented an aspect as singular as any that ever lived upon the face of the earth, all seated in a circle, father, mother, sons and daughters, and giving the most profound attention to a boy."[29] The Smiths had implicit confidence in Joseph. When his brother William was asked if he doubted "Joseph's testimony" he replied, "No we all had implicit confidence in what he said. He was a truthful boy. Father and Mother believed him; why should not the children?"[30]

How did the Smith family deal with the persecution that followed Joseph's heavenly manifestations?

The family remained calm though mocked, ridiculed, and abused. Mother Smith wrote, "Truly ours was a happy family, although persecuted by the preachers, who declared there was no more vision, the canon of scripture was full, and no more revelation was needed."[31]

Was Joseph Smith employed as a money digger?

In the 1820s citizens residing in western New York and Pennsylvania employed magic to search for hidden treasures by unorthodox means. Upright citizens and greedy speculators alike believed that great treasures, even a legendary lost Spanish silver mine, were concealed in the earth. Men scoured the land looking for hidden wealth. Their insatiable desire for riches caused them to abandon farm labor and follow a crazed and frenzied search. With this backdrop, and "on account of having heard that [Joseph] possessed certain means by which he could discern things invisible to the natural eye," he was hired to dig for a lost silver mine in the Oquago Mountain at Harmony, Pennsylvania. Although Joseph "endeavored to divert [his employer] from his vain pursuit," he accepted the terms of employment and in October 1825 went to Harmony to commence digging.[32] "I continued to work for nearly a month, without success in [my] undertaking, and finally I prevailed with the old gentleman to cease digging," wrote Joseph.[33] The digging stopped on November 17, 1825, about one month after it began.

How did Joseph Smith meet his bride, Emma Hale?

The unfruitful dig for hidden treasure unwittingly

brought Joseph closer to the matrimonial altar. As a hired hand for treasure speculators, he boarded with the Isaac Hale family and, "I first saw my wife (his daughter), Emma Hale."[34] His happiness in meeting his future bride was tempered by the cold reception of her father. Joseph attributed the animosity to "my continuing to assert that I had seen a vision."[35] Isaac Hale recalled that Joseph "made several visits at my house, and at length asked my consent to his marrying my daughter Emma. This I refused."[36] Joseph returned to Palmyra, but he could not forget his feelings for Emma. Joseph said to his parents, "I have concluded to get married; and if you have no objections to uniting myself in marriage with Miss Emma Hale, she would be my choice in preference to any other woman I have seen."[37] Emma was married to Joseph on January 18, 1827, in South Bainbridge, New York, by Squire Tarble. "I had no intention of marrying when I left home," Emma wrote, "but [Joseph] urged me to marry him, and preferring to marry him to any other man I knew, I consented."[38] Although Emma knew of her father's feelings toward Joseph, she chose to marry him and exert her adult independence.

When did Joseph Smith receive the ancient record written on gold plates?

Near midnight on September 22, 1827, Joseph climbed the hill in Palmyra where the plates were deposited and there was met by an angel named Moroni who "delivered [the gold plates] up to me with this charge: that I should be responsible for them; that if I should let them go carelessly, or through any neglect of mine, I should be cut off; but that if I would use all my endeavors to preserve them, until he, the messenger, should call for them, they should be protected."[39]

Did Joseph Smith have to physically protect the gold plates?

As word of gold treasure spread from house to house in Palmyra, assailants tried to take what they called Joe's "Gold Bible." Cash and property were offered for a glimpse of the plates. When Joseph refused, schemes were contrived to snatch the treasure. Keeping the plates safe proved difficult for Joseph. A birch log, hearth stones, floor boards, flax, and a barrel of beans were used to keep thieves at bay.

How did Joseph Smith translate the ancient record known as the Book of Mormon?

On November 13, 1843, Joseph wrote a letter to James Arlington Bennett, in which he explained the translation process: "By the power of God I translated the Book of Mormon from hieroglyphics, the knowledge of which was lost to the world, in which wonderful event I stood alone, an unlearned youth, to combat the worldly wisdom and multiplied ignorance of eighteen centuries, with a new revelation."[40]

Did Joseph Smith use scribes while translating the ancient record?

His wife Emma acted as a scribe for a portion of the Book of Mormon translation. She said of her experience, "The Book of Mormon is of divine authenticity—I have not the slightest doubt of it. I am satisfied that no man could have dictated the writing of the manuscripts unless he was inspired; for, when acting as his scribe, [Joseph] would dictate to me hour after hour; and when returning after meals, or after interruptions, he would at once begin where he left off, without either seeing the manuscript or having any portion of it read to him. This was a usual thing for him to do. It would have been improbable that a learned man could do this; and, for one so ignorant and unlearned as he was, it was simply impossible."[41] However, the main scribe for the Book of Mormon was Oliver Cowdery, who testified, "I wrote with my own pen the entire book of mormon (Save a few pages) as it fell from the Lips of the prophet [Joseph Smith]. As he translated [it] by the gift and power of god, By [the] means of the urum and thummim, or as it is called by that book holy Interpreters. I beheld with my eyes. And handled with my hands the gold plates from which it was translated. I also beheld the Interpreters. That book is true. Sidney Rigdon did no write it. Mr [Solomon] Spaulding did not write it. I wrote it myself as it fell from the Lips of the prophet."[42]

When did Joseph Smith and his scribe Oliver Cowdery receive the Aaronic and Melchizedek priesthoods?

While translating the Book of Mormon Joseph had questions about authority to "administer the ordinances of the gospel."[43] Seeking an answer, he and Oliver Cowdery "went into the woods to pray and inquire of the Lord respecting baptism for the remission of sins, that we found mentioned in the translation of the plates." While in prayer on May 15, 1829, near the timber-lined Susquehanna River "a messenger from heaven descended in a cloud of light, and having laid his hands upon us, he ordained us, saying: *Upon you my fellow servants, in the name of Messiah, I confer the Priesthood of Aaron, which holds the keys of the ministering of angels, and of the gospel of repentance, and of baptism.*" The messenger was the prophet John, known in the New Testament as John the Baptist. He commanded Joseph and Oliver "to go and be baptized, and gave us directions that I should baptize Oliver Cowdery, and that afterwards he should baptize me." John the Baptist promised that the priesthood of Melchizedek "would in due time be conferred on us."[44]

In answer to another prayer, ancient apostles—Peter, James and John—restored the Melchizedek Priesthood and the keys of the apostleship to Joseph Smith and Oliver Cowdery.[45] "I was present with Joseph," wrote Oliver on this sacred occasion, "when the higher or Melchizedek Priesthood was conferred by holy angels from on high. This priesthood we then conferred on each other, by the will and commandment of God."[46]

Did anyone besides Joseph Smith see the gold plates and the angel?

Three witnesses—Oliver Cowdery, David Whitmer, and Martin Harris—were shown the ancient engraved plates by an angelic messenger. The testimony of these men is printed in the front pages of the published Book of Mormon, a portion of which reads:

> "Be it known unto all nations, kindreds, tongues, and people, unto whom this work shall come: That we, through the grace of God the Father, and our Lord Jesus Christ, have seen the plates which contain this record, which is a record of the people of Nephi, and also of the Lamanites, their brethren, and also of the people of Jared, who came from the tower of which hath been spoken. And we also know that they have been translated by the gift and power of God, for his voice hath declared it unto us; wherefore we know of a surety that the work is true. And we also testify that we have seen the engravings which are upon the plates; and they have been shown unto us by the power of God, and not of man. And we declare with words of soberness, that an angel of God came down from heaven, and he brought and laid before our eyes, that we beheld and saw the plates, and the engravings thereon."[47]

Did Joseph Smith believe the Book of Mormon was holy scripture?

On November 28, 1841, in a discourse given in Nauvoo, Joseph said, "I told the brethren that the Book of Mormon was the most correct of any book on earth, and the keystone of our religion, and a man would get nearer to God by abiding by its precepts, than by any other book."[48]

When was the Church of Jesus Christ of Latter-day Saints organized?

On Tuesday, April 6, 1830, in the Peter Whitmer Sr. log cabin in Fayette, New York, the organizational meeting of the Church of Jesus Christ of Latter-day Saints was held. The group opened with prayer, emblems of the Savior's sacrifice (bread and wine) were blessed and passed, and "the Holy Ghost was poured out upon us to a very great degree—some prophesied, whilst we all praised the Lord, and rejoiced exceedingly."[49] Those in attendance acknowledged Joseph Smith to be "a seer, a translator, a prophet, an apostle of Jesus Christ, an elder of the church through the will of God the Father, and the grace of your Lord Jesus Christ."[50]

How did this newly formed church grow so quickly?

Those who attended the foundational meeting shared the gospel with friends, pastors, congregations, and strangers who, in turn, talked with near neighbors and distant relatives. Young and old, rich and poor, farmer and educator listened and embraced the teachings of the new sect. Thus, the gospel spread through New York and from there to Ohio.

Why was Joseph Smith so successful in gaining followers?

On July 9, 1843, in a discourse given in Nauvoo, Joseph

said, "Sectarian priests cry out concerning me, and ask 'Why is it this babbler gains so many followers, and retains them?' I answer, it is because I possess the principle of love. All I can offer the world is a good heart and a good hand."[51]

Did Joseph Smith prophecy that membership in the Church of Jesus Christ of Latter-day Saints would be in the millions?

On a Sunday night in April 1834, Joseph Smith "called on all who held the Priesthood to gather into the little log school house they had there. It was a small house, perhaps 14 feet square. But it held the whole of the Priesthood of the Church of Jesus Christ of Latter-day Saints who were then in the town of Kirtland. . . . When we got together the Prophet called upon the Elders of Israel with him to bear testimony of this work. . . . When they got through the Prophet said, 'Brethren I have been very much edified and instructed in your testimonies here tonight, but I want to say before the Lord, that you know no more concerning the destinies of this Church and kingdom than a babe upon its mother's lap. You don't comprehend it.' I was rather surprised. He said 'it is only a little handful of Priesthood you see here tonight, but this Church will fill North and South America—it will fill the world.'"[52]

Why did Joseph Smith encourage his followers to move from western New York to Kirtland, Ohio?

In December 1830, Joseph received a revelation from God commanding his followers to leave western New York "because of the enemy and for your sakes."[53] In obedience, followers sold their houses, out-dwellings, and other possessions to migrate to Ohio. Whatever their economic circumstances, neither poverty nor discomfort stopped the flow of faithful followers to Ohio. So great were their numbers, one journalist announced the "whole world" would soon be living in rural Kirtland. "Every available house, shop, hut, or barn was filled to its utmost capacity. Even boxes were roughly extemporized and used for shelter until something more permanent could be secured."[54]

Are Joseph Smith and his followers credited with building the community of Kirtland, Ohio?

Kirtland was a small agrarian community before Joseph Smith and his followers arrived in 1831. Due to their industry, however, businesses and mercantile establishments sprang up seemingly overnight. Under the name of the new church, a printing office, a bank, and sundry other work places—an ashery, tannery, shoe shop, forge, pottery, steam sawmill, and lumber kiln—became thriving enterprises. "The starting up, as if by magic, of buildings in every direction around us, were evincive to us of buoyant hope, lively anticipation, and a firm confidence that our days of pinching adversity had passed," wrote Oliver Cowdery.[55] To the amazement of near neighbors, Mormons turned Kirtland into a mushrooming community that was larger and according to some, more notable than the Ohio towns of Chardon, Painesville, Akron, Canton, Warren, and Youngstown.

Was Joseph Smith persecuted in Ohio?

Abuse in Ohio was more apparent and unchecked than it had been in western New York. For example, on the eve of March 24, 1832, when Joseph and his wife Emma were caring for their eleven-month-old twins (ill from the effects of measles), a dozen men broke into their bedroom. The intruders grabbed at Joseph's "shirt, drawers and limbs." His struggle to free himself spawned threats of death from the lawless men. "[This] quieted me," Joseph said. "You will have mercy and spare my life, I hope," he pled. The profane response was, "Call on yer

God for help, we'll show ye no mercy." They "beat and scratch me well, tear off my shirt and drawers, and leave me naked," Joseph said. Tar and feathers followed—feathers symbolizing that these men openly mocked Joseph Smith and his teachings. Confident that their dark deed had left their victim dead, they scattered into the shadows of the night. Joseph did not die that night, but he was unconscious when the mobbers fled. When consciousness returned, he cautiously moved toward the farmhouse from which he had been dragged. Once inside the house, Joseph's distraught followers carefully removed tar from his "scarified and defaced" body. The next day, Joseph preached as usual. In a letter written to Bishop Partridge on December 5, 1838, Joseph wrote of his confidence amid persecution: "Our trust is in God, and we are determined, His grace assisting us, to maintain the cause and hold out faithful unto the end."[56]

Did Joseph Smith attempt to translate the Bible?

Joseph believed that "many important points touching the salvation of man, had been taken from the Bible, or lost before it was compiled." As he read the Bible, the missing scriptural passages were revealed to him by the Lord. "Could you gaze into heaven five minutes, you would know more than you would by reading all that ever was written on this subject," he said.[57] For example, as he was translating John 5:29, Joseph and his scribe, Sidney Rigdon, saw in vision God the Father and Jesus Christ and testified, "After the many testimonies which have been given of him, this is the testimony, last of all, which we give of him: That he lives! For we saw him, even on the right hand of God; and we heard the voice bearing record that he is the Only Begotten of the Father."[58] Joseph's "new translation," as he called it, was published after his death. However, the "new translation" proved to be the impetus for numerous revelations that shaped much of the church's doctrine. Many of the revelations are published in the Doctrine and Covenants.

Did Joseph Smith claim to have daily revelations from God?

At the death of Lorenzo D. Barnes on April 15, 1843, Joseph said, "It is my meditation all the day, and more than my meat and drink, to know how I shall make the Saints of God comprehend the visions that roll like an overflowing surge before my mind."[59]

Did Joseph Smith lead a militia to Missouri?

When Joseph received word that his followers in Jackson County, Missouri, had been forced from their homes, he sent an immediate reply to the religious exiles: "Your sufferings, it awakens every sympathy of our hearts; it weighs us down; we cannot refrain from tears, yet, we are not able to realize, only in part, your sufferings." Hoping to relieve the suffering, Joseph rallied the strength of the Ohio Saints and formed a quasi-military force known as Zion's Camp. During the early days of the march toward Missouri, he wrote, "God was with us, and his angels went before us, and the faith of our little band was unwavering." Yet, as the days extended to weeks, failure of camp members to heed divine warnings provoked the wrath of God. Infectious cholera spread quickly through the camp. Sixty-eight members of the group (in total 207) succumbed to the illness and thirteen died. Failing to halt the spreading plague, Joseph wrote in a letter to Edward Partridge and others on December 10, 1833 that he "learned by painful experience, that when the great Jehovah decrees destruction upon any people, and makes known His determination, man must not attempt to stay His hand."[60] The bleak vexation and subsequent dispersion of Zion's Camp offered little promise to the exiled Jacksonian Saints.

Did future church leaders emerge during Zion's Camp?

On Saturday, February 14, 1835, a meeting was held in a schoolhouse in Kirtland for all "those who journeyed last season to Zion for the purpose of laying the foundation of its redemption, together with as many other of the brethren and sisters as were disposed to attend." The schoolhouse was crowded to overflowing in anticipation of the camp reunion even before Joseph arrived. As the presiding officer and former leader of Zion's Camp, Joseph called the meeting to order and read passages from the 15th chapter of John. He then said, "Let us endeavor to solemnize our minds that we may receive a blessing, by calling on the Lord. After an appropriate and affecting prayer, the brethren who went to Zion [in Zion's camp] were requested to take their seats together in a part of the house by themselves." Joseph stated that this meeting was different than other reunions for it had been called of God and "made known to him by vision and by the Holy Spirit" for "those who went to Zion, with a determination to lay down their lives, if necessary, should be ordained to the ministry, and go forth to prune the vineyard for the last time, or the coming of the Lord, which was nigh."

Joseph spoke specifically on the "subject of choosing the Twelve, wanted an expression from the brethren, if they would be satisfied to have the Spirit of the Lord dictate in the choice of the Elders to be Apostles; whereupon all the Elders present expressed their anxious desire to have it so." The "first business of the meeting was, for the Three Witnesses of the Book of Mormon to pray, each one, and then proceed to choose twelve men from the Church, as Apostles, to go to all nations, kindreds, tongues, and people." The witnesses—Oliver Cowdery, David Whitmer, and Martin Harris—united in prayer before the First Presidency—Joseph Smith Jr., Sidney Rigdon, and

Frederick G. Williams. The presidency then laid hands upon the heads of the witnesses and set them apart to select and ordain twelve men to be the especial witnesses or Apostles of the Lord Jesus Christ. According to directions, after having sat in counsel with the First Presidency, the Three Witnesses named: 1) Lyman E. Johnson, 2) Brigham Young, 3) Heber C. Kimball, 4) Orson Hyde, 5) David W. Patten, 6) Luke S. Johnson, 7) William E. M'Lellin, 8) John F. Boynton, 9) Orson Pratt, 10) William Smith, 11) Thomas B. Marsh, and 12) Parley P. Pratt.

Were members of Zion's Camp angry when the camp was dispersed without returning Jacksonian exiles to their lands?

After Joseph Smith returned to Ohio, a few camp members accused him "with a catalogue of charges as black as the author of lies himself" for unbecoming conduct in Zion's Camp. Cries of "Tyrant—Pope—King—Usurper—Abuser" were shouted in a spirit of contention and apostasy.[61] Acquitted of any wrongdoing, Joseph forgave his accusers. The accusers, however, were not appeased. They aligned themselves with a growing mob element in Kirtland.

Why did Joseph Smith and his followers build a temple?

In Kirtland, the Lord revealed to Joseph the importance of building "a house, even a house of prayer, a house of fasting, a house of faith, a house of learning, a house of glory, a house of order, a house of God"—a temple.[62] When Joseph shared the revelation with his followers, one suggested that the temple be a wood-framed building and another, a log structure. "Shall we, brethren, build a house for our God, of logs?" Joseph asked. "No," he replied, "I have a better plan than that. I have a plan of the house of the Lord, given by himself."[63] The plan was intricate in detail and magnificent in design, but it was financially beyond the reach of the poverty-stricken Latter-day Saints. "Notwithstanding the Church was poor," Joseph observed, his followers began to build.[64] Work on the temple commenced on June 5, 1833. By the summer of that year, nearly every able-bodied follower of Joseph had contributed time and labor to build on the temple. From cutting stones to felling trees, and milling to skilled carpentry, they worked night and day at a hurried pace to construct a temple that would glorify God. "There was but one mainspring to all our thoughts and actions, and that was, the building of the Lord's house," declared Mother Smith.[65] The reason the building was so important to the Latter-day Saints was that it would become a house of the Lord in which they could worship God and make sacred covenants.

Were Kirtland residents pleased with the temple?

Followers of Joseph believed that each stone added to the temple walls stirred neighbors' agitation to new heights. By the winter of 1833–34, mobs threatened to tear down the walls and kill the Latter-day prophet. For weeks Joseph's followers did not remove their work clothes and "gave no sleep to their eyes, nor slumber to their eyelids" to protect the temple walls and the life of their leader. "Our enemies were raging and threatening destruction upon us," Heber C. Kimball recalled. "[We] were obliged to lie with our fire-locks in our arms, to preserve Brother Joseph's life."[66] "Notwithstanding the threats of the mob," said Joseph, temple construction went steadily forward.[67]

Was the Kirtland Temple dedicated to God?

The Kirtland Temple was dedicated on March 27, 1836. To Benjamin Brown, a convert, the dedication was "as on the day of Pentecost, [the Holy Ghost] was profusely poured out. Hundreds of Elders spoke in tongues. . . . We had a most glorious and never-to-be-forgotten time. Angels were seen by numbers present."[68] The congregation sang,

> The Spirit of God like a fire is burning!
> The latter-day glory begins to come forth;
> The visions and blessings of old are returning,
> And angels are coming to visit the earth.[69]

The heavens were opened, visions were seen, and the Saints shouted, "Hosannah, to God and the Lamb." They sealed their shout with a united "Amen."[70]

Did Joseph Smith see Jesus Christ in the Kirtland Temple?

In the afternoon of April 3, 1836, Joseph recalled, "I retired to the pulpit [in the Kirtland Temple], the veils being dropped, and bowed myself, with Oliver Cowdery, in solemn and silent prayer." While praying, "the veil was taken from our minds, and the eyes of our understanding were opened. We saw the Lord standing upon the breastwork of the pulpit, before us; and under his feet was a paved work of pure gold, in color like amber. His eyes were as a flame of fire; the hair of his head was white like the pure snow; his countenance shone above the brightness of the sun; and his voice was as the sound of the rushing of great waters, even the voice of Jehovah." Joseph and his scribe Oliver Cowdery heard the Savior say, "I have accepted this house . . . And the fame of this house shall spread to foreign lands; and this is the beginning of the blessing which shall be poured out upon the heads of my people."[71]

What impact did the nationwide banking crisis in 1837 have on Joseph Smith and his followers?

The Kirtland Safety Society Anti-Banking Company,

which Joseph helped found, failed like many other banks nationwide. The failure caused some Latter-day Saints to waver and reconsider their faith. Several joined with the mob element in Kirtland and sought to "destroy the Prophet Joseph and his followers." Benjamin Johnson wrote, "And it almost seemed to me that the brightest stars in our firmament had fallen."[72] Joseph concurred: "It seemed as though all the powers of earth and hell were combining their influence in an especial manner to overthrow the Church at once, and make a final end."[73] The division created within the community proved advantageous to anti-Mormons, whose "fruitful imaginations were aroused to the utmost, to invent new schemes to accomplish our destruction."[74] Persecution became so violent that Joseph "regarded it as unsafe to remain any longer in Kirtland, and began to make arrangements to move to Missouri."[75] Faithful Saints followed his example. "What the Lord will do with us I know not," wrote John Smith, "altho he slay me I will trust in him. We are like the ancients wandering from place to place in the wilderness."[76]

How was Joseph Smith received among his followers in Missouri?

When Joseph arrived in Missouri, after hiding in wagons "to elude the grasp of pursuers who . . . [were] armed with pistols and guns," he was greeted with mixed emotions. Faithful church members expressed joy: "Many of the brethren came out to meet us, who also with open arms welcomed us to their bosoms." The disillusioned remained aloof, but they secretly whispered innuendos that disclosed their contempt. As slanderous hearsay spread, attempts to establish truth were summarily dismissed as falsehoods. Solomon Hancock's unwavering testimony given on December 13, 1838, "Brother Joseph is not a fallen prophet, but will yet be exalted and become very high," almost went unnoticed amid vexatious lawsuits, name-calling, and the betrayal of the Mormon leader.[77]

Were Joseph Smith's followers prepared for additional persecution in Missouri?

Followers of Joseph, who joined him in Missouri, hoped the tribulations they had experienced in Ohio were behind them. Yet tales of prejudice and hatred stemming from the growth of Mormonism in Missouri sounded all too familiar. Bishop Edward Partridge bearing "abuse with so much resignation and meekness, that it appeared to astound the multitude, who permitted me to retire in silence, many looking very solemn, their sympathies having been touched," was reminiscent of Ohio scenes.[78] Likewise Levi Hancock's words, "All my property was scattered to the four winds, tools and all for pretended claims, where I owed not one cent justly" were also familiar.[79] And Joseph Knight's description of "submit[ting] to the numerous indignities heaped upon us, . . . [and] made many concessions to the mob in hope of pacifying them, but it was useless," sounded as if he had spoken the words in Ohio.[80]

What communities did Joseph Smith and his people build in northern Missouri?

In spite of outward challenges, Joseph counseled his followers to build the communities of Far West, DeWitt, and Adam-ondi-Ahman. Latter-day Saints listened and obeyed. They transformed rolling Missouri prairies into enterprising communities. Shops, mercantile establishments, and hundreds of log homes were the fruits of their labors.

What was the "extermination order" against Latter-day Saints in the state of Missouri?

On October 27, 1838, Missouri Governor Lilburn W.

Boggs issued an extermination order against the Latter-day Saints: "The Mormons must be treated as enemies and *must be exterminated* or driven from the state, if necessary for the public good." Mormon "outrages are beyond all description," the governor penned.[81] A massacre in the Mormon community of Haun's Mill and the fall of DeWitt stemmed from this executive decree. Joseph Smith's brother Hyrum "endeavored to find out for what cause" the Latter-day Saints were subjected to such violence and death. "All we could learn was, that it was because we were 'Mormons,'" said Hyrum.[82] The executive order put in harm's way every man, woman, and child who would not deny that Joseph Smith was a prophet.

Where did Mormons settle after the extermination order?

Seeking refuge, Joseph Smith's followers traveled east, fording the icy Mississippi River. Witnessing the Mormons cross the mighty river was Illinois attorney O. H. Browning: "Great God! have I not seen it? Yes, my eyes have beheld the blood-stained traces of innocent women and children, in the drear winter, who had traveled hundreds of miles barefoot, through frost and snow, to seek a refuge from their savage pursuers."[83] Among their number was Titus Billings, who wrote, "Never have had a writ served upon me not broken the law in one instance and now I say that these things have come upon us on account of the religion which we profess."[84] Billings and other Mormon exiles settled near the Mississippi in the river town of Quincy, Illinois.

Did Joseph Smith escape extreme persecution in Missouri?

Joseph and his closest associates surrendered to military generals outside the confines of the Mormon community of Far West. The Mormon leaders did so believing there was "no alternative but to put ourselves into the hands of such monsters, or to have the city attacked, and men, women and children massacred." During the long evening hours that followed, military guards "kept up a constant tirade of mockery, and the most obscene blackguardism and abuse. They blasphemed God; mocked Jesus Christ; swore the most dreadful oaths; taunted brother Joseph and others; demanded miracles; wanted signs, such as: 'Come, Mr. Smith, show us an angel.' 'Give us one of your revelations.' 'Show us a miracle.'"[85] In answer to the mockery, Joseph and his fellow captives fell silent.

Why was a military court martial held against the Mormon prisoners?

On November 1, 1838, a court martial was held to determine the fate of Joseph Smith and his fellow captives. Fourteen Missouri militia officers, twenty preachers, and a few local judges were present. When the court ended near midnight, General Samuel Lucas issued an execution order and commanded General Alexander Doniphan and his militia to kill the prisoners: "Sir:—You will take Joseph Smith and the other prisoners into the public square of Far West, and shoot them at 9 o'clock tomorrow morning." Doniphan refused to comply: "It is cold blooded murder. I will not obey your order," he penned. "If you execute these men, I will hold you responsible before an earthly tribunal, so help me God!" Doniphan's defiance "so alarmed the haughty murderer and his accomplices that they dare not put the decree in execution."[86]

Rather than free the prisoners after the court martial, General Lucas and the Jackson County militia took the Mormon prisoners to Independence. Along the route, a feeling of doom overcame the captives until Joseph whispered, *Be of good cheer, brethren; the word of the Lord came to me last night that our lives should be given us, and that whatever we may suffer during this captivity, not one of our lives should be taken.*"[87] Many curiosity seekers clamored to see the Mormon leaders as the wagons neared Independence on November 4, 1838. "Which of the prisoners [is] the Lord whom the 'Mormons' worship?" a woman asked. When a soldier pointed to Joseph, she approached him and inquired "whether [he] professed to be the Lord and Savior?" Joseph replied, "I professed to be nothing but a man, and a minister of salvation, sent by Jesus Christ to preach the Gospel."[88] He then preached the doctrines of faith, repentance, baptism, and the Holy Ghost. "All seemed surprised, and the lady, in tears, went her way, praising God for the truth, and praying aloud that the Lord would bless and deliver the prisoners."[89]

What was Joseph Smith's experience in the Independence Jail?

Joseph and his fellow prisoners were visited by "hundreds [of people who] flocked to see us day after day. We spent most of our time in [Independence Jail] preaching and convers[ing], explanatory of our doctrines and practice. Much prejudice was removed, and the feelings of the populace began to be in our favor, notwithstanding their former wickedness and hatred."[90]

How did Joseph Smith react to continued captivity?

On December 16, 1838, Joseph wrote to church members in Caldwell County, Missouri, "Dear brethren, do not think that our hearts faint, as though some strange things had happened unto us, for we have seen and been assured of all these things beforehand, and have an assurance of a better hope than that of our persecutors. Therefore God hath made broad our shoulders for the burden. We glory in our tribulations, because we know that God is with us, that He is our friend, and that He will save our souls. We do not care for them that can kill the body; they cannot harm our souls. We ask no favors at the hands of mobs, nor of the world, nor of the devil, nor of his emissaries the dissenters, and those who love, and make, and swear falsehoods, to take away our lives. We have never dissembled, nor will we for the sake of our lives."[91]

Did extreme persecution against Mormons in Missouri halt the spread of Mormonism?

On March 1, 1842, Joseph Smith wrote to John Wentworth, "Persecution has not stopped the progress of truth, but has only added fuel to the flame, it has spread with increasing rapidity. . . . The Standard of Truth has been erected; no unhallowed hand can stop the work from progressing; persecutions may rage, mobs may combine, armies may assemble, calumny may defame, but the truth of God will go forth boldly, nobly, and independent, till it has penetrated every continent, visited every clime, swept every country, and sounded in every ear, till the purposes of God shall be accomplished, and the Great Jehovah shall say the work is done."[92]

Was Joseph Smith's imprisonment in Richmond Jail similar to his experience in Independence Jail?

After a brief confinement in Independence, Joseph and the other prisoners were escorted to Richmond, Missouri, by military guards. On November 10, 1838, they were confined in a ramshackled log cabin in Richmond. Their legs were chained and padlocked by the state prison keeper, while guards kept guns pointed at them. Joseph described the chains that bound the prisoners as being "bound together in chains as well as the cords of everlasting love, we are in good spirits and rejoice that we are counted worthy to be persecuted for Christ sake."[93] Common courtesies, such as providing utensils for eating, were denied them. Joseph's distress from a toothache and a fever caused by exposure to cold weather was ignored by the guards. Adding to their problems was the profane cursing and taunting of their captors.

Was it in Richmond Jail that Joseph rebuked prison guards?

Parley P. Pratt wrote, "I had listened till I became so disgusted, shocked, horrified, and so filled with the spirit of indignant justice that I could scarcely refrain from rising upon my feet and rebuking the guards." However, he was not the one to silence them. He wrote of Joseph arising to his feet and speaking with "a voice of thunder, or as the roaring lion, . . . '*SILENCE, ye fiends of the infernal pit. In the name of Jesus Christ I rebuke you, and command you to be still; I will not live another minute and hear such language. Cease such talk, or you or I die THIS INSTANT!*'" Parley explained that Joseph stood "in terrible majesty. Chained, and without a weapon; calm, unruffled and dignified." There was such a tone of finality in Joseph's words, such a commanding authority in his bearing, that the "quailing guards, whose weapons were lowered or dropped to the ground; whose knees smote together, and who, shrinking into a corner, or crouching at his feet, begged his pardon, and remained quiet till a change of guards."[94]

What happened at the Richmond court hearing?

The civil hearing in Richmond, often referred to as a "mock trial," began on November 12, 1838. The honorable Austin A. King, fifth judicial circuit court judge, presided. King welcomed crowds of spectators into the unfurnished courthouse to observe the proceedings. The hostile audience, convinced that the prisoners were guilty, intimidated witnesses and defendants throughout the hearing. One man shouted, "There is a red hot Mormon, d-mn him, I am acquainted with him."

Another blurted out, "That dam rascal was in the battle—or out to Davis—or to De-Wit, such a one is a great preacher and leader amongst them, he ought to be hung, or sent to the penitentiary." Judge King made no attempt to quell the outbursts. Even when one of the prison guards shouted, "Shoot your Mormon, I have shot mine," King remained unruffled.[95] The fourteen-day hearing focused on alleged Mormon raiding expeditions in northern Missouri counties and the suspected treason of Mormon leaders. The prosecution called forty-one witnesses; twenty Missourians and twenty-one dissenting Mormons. Forty or fifty names of defense witnesses were submitted to Judge King. He turned the list over to a militia captain for further arrests. A second attempt resulted in the same charade. Only seven witnesses—four men and three women—evaded the court intimidations and testified on behalf of the prisoners. On the basis of the evidence presented, Judge King found probable cause to order Joseph Smith and others to Liberty Jail on charges of overt acts of treason.

What were Joseph Smith's experiences in Liberty Jail?

The day after Judge Austin A. King gavelled the hearing to a close, six prisoners, including Joseph Smith, were chained, cuffed, placed in a wagon, and taken to the town of Liberty. On December 1, 1838, they were locked in the squalor of Liberty Jail. "Our place of lodging was the square side of hewed white oak logs, and our food was anything but good and decent," wrote Hyrum Smith, Joseph's brother and fellow prisoner. "Poison was administered to us three or four times. . . . The poison would inevitably have proved fatal had not the power of Jehovah interposed in our behalf, to save us from their wicked purpose."[96] The prisoners petitioned the supreme court of Missouri twice for a writ of habeas corpus, but they were denied. Unofficially, they were told *"There was no law for the Mormons in the State of Missouri.*"[97] Joseph concluded, "The soldiers and officers of every kind hated us, and the most profane blasphemers and drunkards & whoremongers hated us, they all hated us most cordially. And now what did they hate us for, purely because of the testimony of Jesus Christ."[98]

From Liberty Jail, Joseph penned letters of encouragement to his wife and friends. To his wife, Emma, Joseph wrote, "As to yourself if you want to know how much I want to see you, examine your feelings, how much you want to see me, and Judge for yourself, I would gladly walk from here to you barefoot, and bareheaded, and half naked, to see you and think it great pleasure."[99] A few months later, he wrote, "Dear Emma I very well know your toils and sympathize with you if God will spare my life once more to have the privilege of taking care of you I will ease your care and endeavor to comfort your heart." He admonished her to "not let those little fellows, to forget me, tell them Father loves them with a perfect love, and he is doing all he can to get away from the mob to come to them."[100] To his friends, who had escaped from Missouri, the Mormon leader wrote counsel, direction, and assurance of the omnipotent power of God: "What power shall stay the heavens? As well might man stretch forth his puny arm to stop the Missouri river in its decreed course, or to turn it up stream, as to hinder the Almighty from pouring down knowledge from heaven upon the heads of the Latter-day Saints."[101] When hope seemed only a glimmer, Joseph cried, "O God, where art thou? And where is the pavilion that covereth thy hiding place? How long shall thy hand be stayed, and thine eye, yea thy pure eye, behold from the eternal heavens the wrongs of thy people and of thy servants, and thine ear be penetrated with their cries?" The Lord comforted Joseph: "My son, peace be unto thy soul; thine adversity and thine afflictions shall be but a small moment; And then, if thou endure it well, God shall exalt thee on high; thou shalt triumph over all thy foes. Thy friends do stand by thee, and they shall hail thee again with warm hearts and friendly hands. Thou are not yet as Job; thy friends do not contend against thee, neither charge thee with transgression, as they did Job. . . . if the very jaws of hell shall gape open the mouth wide after thee, know thou, my son, that all these things shall give thee experience, and shall be for thy good. The Son of Man hath descended below them all. Art thou greater than he? . . . fear not what man can do, for God shall be with you forever and ever."[102]

How did Joseph escape from Liberty Jail?

Freedom was granted to the Latter-day Saint prophet and his fellow prisoners by a most unusual turn of events. In April of 1839, they were awarded a change of venue to Boone County, Missouri. While they were being transported, the prison guards became intoxicated. "We thought it a favorable opportunity to make our escape," wrote Joseph. Rather than the change prescribed by Missouri law, Hyrum Smith said, "We took our change of venue for the state of Illinois."[103] Upon arriving in Quincy, they were lovingly embraced by family and friends. Parley P. Pratt, a fellow prisoner who had also escaped, wrote of greeting Joseph in Illinois: "Neither of us could refrain from tears as we embraced each other once more as free men. We felt like shouting hosannah in the highest, and giving glory to that God who had delivered us in fulfilment of His word."[104]

Did Joseph Smith's followers help him withstand so many difficulties?

In a July 1840 letter to Oliver Granger, Joseph penned, "As long as my brethren stand by me and encourage me, I can combat the prejudices of the world, and can bear the contumely [harsh treatment] and abuse with joy; but when my brethren stand aloof, when they begin to faint, and endeavor to retard my progress and enterprise, then I feel to mourn, but am no less determined to prosecute my task, being confident that although my earthly friends may fail, and even turn against me, yet my heavenly Father will bear me off triumphant."[105]

Did Joseph Smith appeal to the president of the United States for help?

In February of 1840, Joseph and other Mormon leaders traveled to Washington, D.C. to put before President Martin Van Buren "Missouri Redress Petitions," which itemized the wrongs Mormons had endured in Missouri. President Van Buren concluded, "Gentlemen, *Your cause is just, but I can do nothing for you.* If I take up for you I shall lose the vote of Missouri."[106]

When did Joseph Smith settle his followers in the swampland of Commerce, Illinois?

By April 1839, Joseph was determined to find a place of refuge—a place where his people could worship God without threats of persecution. Near an unlikely bluff overlooking a swampy bend in the Mississippi River, such a place was presented to him. Land speculators offered to sell the mosquito-infested marshlands, called Commerce, for almost no money down. Mormon exiles could afford very little, so the purchase price was acceptable. In describing the purchase Joseph said, "The place was literally a wilderness. The land was mostly covered with trees and bushes, and much of it so wet that it was with the utmost difficulty a footman could get through, and totally impossible for teams." Yet with "no more eligible place presenting itself," the prophet "considered it wisdom to make an attempt to build up a city."[107] By May, 1839, Joseph and his family—along with thousands of church members—had settled in Commerce.

Did Latter-day Saints suffer from disease in Commerce?

Weakened by their physically taxing ordeals in Missouri and living in makeshift tents and wagons in Illinois, thousands of Latter-day Saints fell prey to illnesses inherent in the Mississippi Valley. With illness and death on every side, Joseph questioned whether he would succumb. He sought the answer from his father, a patriarch in the church: "You shall even live to finish your work," said his father. Joseph cried out, "Oh! my father, shall I?""Yes," said his father, "you shall live to lay out the plan of all the work which God has given you to do."[108] As to Joseph's willingness to help his followers at this sickly time, Wilford Woodruff recalled, "It was a very sickly time; Joseph had given up his home in Commerce to the sick, and had a tent pitched in his dooryard and was living in that himself."[109] Joseph said, "My house has been a home and resting-place for thousands, and my family many times obliged to do without food, after having fed all they had to visitors." To remedy the problem of feeding so many, one man suggested to Emma Smith, "You must do as [Napoleon] Bonaparte did—have a little table, just large enough for the victuals you want yourself." Emma replied, "Mr. Smith is a bigger man than Bonaparte: he can never eat without his friends."[110]

Did Joseph Smith heal the sick in Commerce?

One example of his using priesthood to heal the sick occurred on the morning of July 22, 1839. Joseph called upon the Lord in mighty prayer for the gift to heal his loved ones. That gift was bestowed upon him throughout the day. By laying hands on the sick, he healed all in his household and those lying in tents in his yard. As he walked among the sick near the Mississippi River, he asked God, in the name of Jesus Christ, that they be restored to health. This request was granted. Joseph then crossed the river to Iowa to bless his followers lying ill near that river bank. Elijah Fordham recalled that Joseph came to his bedside and asked, "Brother Fordham, do you not know me?" Elijah did not respond. Joseph again asked, "Elijah, do you not know me?" A faintly whispered "Yes," was heard. "Have you not faith to be healed?" Joseph asked. "I am afraid it is too late; if you had come sooner, I think I might have been," Elijah said. The Prophet then queried, "Do you believe that Jesus is the Christ?" Meekly, he replied, "I do, Brother Joseph." In a commanding voice Joseph said, "Elijah, I command you, in the name of Jesus of Nazareth, to arise and be made whole."[111] Elijah arose from his bed, dressed, ate, and followed Joseph into the street, watching as he blessed others.

Did Mormons build Nauvoo?

With hammer, saw, trowel, and shovel, the Latter-day Saints replaced the squalor of make-shift tents and log cottages with permanent structures in Commerce, now known as Nauvoo. Home and shop next to barn and stable with a family garden in between was soon the norm. Joseph Smith had told settlers along the Mississippi River that he "would build up a city."[112] The city became known as "The City Beautiful" and contrasted with the meandering river as its inhabitants built grist mills, lumber mills, potteries, tanneries, brickyards, bakeries, and dozens of other home industries that surprised the erstwhile observer. "Nauvoo grew, with magic rapidity, from a few rude homes to a magnificent city," wrote diarist Harvey Cluff. "Houses increased in number, farms were opened up and prairie lands east of the city converted into prosperous fields of golden grain."[113] Tinsmith, baker, cobbler and potter were all hard at work. J. H. Buckingham, a gentleman from Boston, penned, "No one can visit Nauvoo, and come away without a conviction that . . . the body of the Mormons were an industrious, hard-working, and frugal people. In the history of the whole world there cannot be found such another instance of so rapid a rise of a city out of the wilderness—a city so well built, a territory so well cultivated."[114]

Who was the architect of the well planned community of Nauvoo?

Chief architect of the wetlands transformation was Joseph Smith. Under his direction, Mormon craftsmen, artisans, and skilled laborers tamed a swamp, reclaimed a wilderness, built a progressive community from the flats to the bluffs, and created a legendary city that was spoken of with envy as the "Jewel of the Mississippi." They built a light of the world, a city set upon a hill, a community of "singular and most striking beauty"— they built Nauvoo.[115]

The mere fact that the Mormons were succeeding on a swamp when contemporaries in advantaged eastern cities were destitute was unique, if not frustrating, to critical visitors. "Sadly . . . was I disappointed," wrote Reverend Samuel Prior after his visit to Nauvoo. "Instead of seeing a few miserable log cabins and mud hovels, which I had expected to find, I was surprised to see one of the most romantic places that I have visited in the West. The buildings, though many of them were small and of wood, bore the marks of neatness which I have not seen equaled in this country."[116]

When did Joseph Smith introduce the doctrine of baptism for the dead?

On August 15, 1840, at the funeral of Seymour Brunson, Joseph spoke on the subject of baptism for the dead. By September of 1840 such baptisms were being performed in the Mississippi River. Work on a baptismal font for the Nauvoo Temple was begun in the spring of 1841. On November 21,

1841, a temporary wooden font was dedicated. It is estimated that Joseph and his followers did over fifteen thousand baptismal ordinances for deceased loved ones.

What other ordinances did Joseph Smith introduce?

On May 4, 1842, in the upper story of his Red Brick Store, Joseph introduced an ordinance known as the temple endowment. During his lifetime, the Nauvoo Temple was under construction, so endowments were not given in that building. On December 10, 1845, about eighteen months after Joseph's death, the first endowments were performed in the Nauvoo Temple.

Who was the architect of the Nauvoo Temple?

Of all the buildings constructed in Nauvoo, none was as magnificent as the Nauvoo Temple. "I am not capacitated to build according to the world," Joseph Smith told the *Pittsburgh Gazette* editor. Joseph admitted he knew "nothing about architecture and all that." Yet, he had definite ideas about how the Nauvoo Temple should be constructed. To architect William Weeks he said, "I wish you to carry out my designs. I have seen in vision the splendid appearance of that building illuminated, and will have it built according to the pattern shown me."[117] While Weeks struggled to draw the architectural renderings to the specifications of the vision, workers began quarrying limestone for the walls.

Who labored on the Nauvoo Temple?

Joseph Smith worked alongside other workers on the temple. However, his labors were often interrupted. "Brother Joseph talk to us" was a common request and a gospel conversation then followed. "I could lean back and listen. Ah what pleasure this gave me," wrote Wandle Mace. "[The Prophet] would unravel the scriptures and explain doctrine as no other man could. What had been mystery he made so plain it was no longer mystery."[118] Laborers from every state in the union and from nations across the sea came to help build the Nauvoo Temple. The architect with his sand shaker box and the laborer with a chisel or wedge were seen working daily on the temple site. Those carrying gauging tools, turning pegs, wooden mallets, and block planes commonly shared their expertise with novices. No one with a willing heart and a capacity for work was turned away, not even those who lacked tools.

Did the building of the Nauvoo Temple drain public resources?

"Some say it is better to give to the poor than build the Temple," said Joseph Smith on October 15, 1843. He countered "the building of the Temple has sustained the poor who were driven from Missouri, and kept them from starving; and it has been the best means for this object which could be devised."[119]

Did temple builders quit when harassment and persecution threatened them?

When harassment and persecution threatened in the winter of 1843–44, workers continued building activities. When calls for Joseph Smith's death grew loud and Thomas Sharp, editor of the *Warsaw Signal*, trumpeted, "Joe Smith is not safe out of Nauvoo. We would not be surprised to hear of his death by violent means in a short time," workers continued building.[120]

Was Joseph Smith ever free from persecution?

On June 4, 1839, Joseph said, "My enemies endeavored to take every advantage of me. . . . heaping up abuse, getting up vexatious lawsuits, and stirring up the minds of the people against me and the people with whom I was connected, although we had done nothing to deserve such treatment, but were busily engaged in our several vocations, and desirous to live on peaceable and friendly terms with all men. In consequence of such threats and abuse which I was continually subject to, my family were kept in a continual state of alarm, not knowing any morning what would befall me from day to day, particularly when I went from home."[121] He added, "I have learned by experience that the enemy of truth does not slumber, nor cease his exertions to bias the minds of communities against the servants of the Lord, by stirring up the indignation of men upon all matters of importance or interest."[122]

How did Joseph Smith treat his followers?

The widow of Robert Thompson wrote of Joseph's kindness, "I can never forget the tender sympathy and brotherly kindness [Joseph] ever showed toward me and my fatherless child. When riding with him and his wife Emma in their carriage I have known him to alight and gather prairie flowers for my little girl."[123]

How did Joseph Smith treat his wife Emma?

Joseph loved Emma and was not above assisting her. "Emma began to be sick with fever; consequently I kept in the house with her all day," he wrote in his journal on October 29, 1842.[124] At a party held at their home, twenty-one guests "sat down to the dinner-table, and Emma and myself waited on them," Joseph wrote.[125] One Latter-day Saint, observing Joseph doing "woman's work" on January 18, 1843, concluded that mismanagement of home chores by Emma was the root of the domestic problems. "I said to him, Brother Joseph, my wife does more hard work than does your wife." Joseph replied, "If a man cannot learn in this life to appreciate a wife and do his duty by her, in properly taking care of her, he need not expect to be given one in the hereafter." The judgmental advisor wrote, "His words shut my mouth as tight as a clam. I took them as terrible reproof. After that I tried to do better by the good wife I had and tried to lighten her labors."[126]

How did Joseph Smith describe himself?

In May 1843, Joseph said, "I am like a huge, rough stone rolling down from a high mountain; and the only polishing I get is when some corner gets rubbed off . . . all hell knocking off a corner here and a corner there. Thus I will become a smooth and polished shaft in the quiver of the Almighty."[127]

When did the tentative peace in Nauvoo end?

In the winter of 1843–44, ridicule, arrest warrants, and evil speaking accelerated as Mormon apostates searched for ways to thwart Mormon plans and malign the character of the Prophet. Doctrines declared sacred by Joseph Smith were distorted to disprove his claims to divine revelation and arouse the hostile public sentiment to new heights. To Mormons and anti-Mormons alike, an open conflict between citizens of Nauvoo and neighbors in outlying communities seemed the only alternative to solve escalating contention. Gun salesmen, believing the conflict inevitable, tried to entice Mormons to buy weapons to defend themselves against eminent danger. "Don't buy [weapons]," Joseph counseled his followers. "It would be better to buy ploughshares and raise corn with them. . . . Let us keep cool as a cucumber on a frosty morning."[128]

How did Joseph Smith react to his enemies in Carthage?

By June of 1844, Carthage bulged with malcontents. Yet Joseph remained calm. He was confident that "all the enemies upon the face of the earth may roar and exert all their power to bring about my death, but they can accomplish nothing, unless some who are among us and enjoy our society, . . . join with our enemies." He knew that his "life [was] more in danger from some little dough-head of a fool in this city than from all my numerous and inveterate enemies abroad. I am exposed to far greater danger from traitors among ourselves than from enemies without. . . . *we have a Judas in our midst.*"[129]

What charges were made against Joseph Smith in the *Nauvoo Expositor*?

The first and only issue of the *Nauvoo Expositor* newspaper charged Joseph with indulging in whoredoms and abusing political power. It branded him as a base seducer, a liar, and a murderer. To Mother Smith it seemed the *Expositor*, "belched forth the most intolerable and the blackest lies that were ever palmed upon a community."[130] In his role as mayor of Nauvoo, Joseph called a meeting of the Nauvoo city council to discuss the libelous accusations. The council declared the newspaper a public nuisance and authorized a local sheriff to stop all future publications. The swift, destructive actions of the sheriff and his posse led proprietors of the paper to charge Joseph and the city council with starting a riot that led to the demise of their newspaper.

Did Thomas Sharp suggest that Joseph Smith be killed?

Thomas Sharp, editor of the *Warsaw Signal*, printed an inflammatory accusation: "War and extermination is inevitable!" He encouraged residents of Warsaw and Carthage to take up arms and destroy Nauvoo, "CITIZENS ARISE, ONE AND ALL!!! Can you stand by, and suffer such INFERNAL DEVILS! to rob men of their property and RIGHTS, without avenging them. We have no time for comment; every man will make his own. LET IT BE MADE WITH POWDER AND BALL!!!"[131] The inescapable target of Sharp's proposed extermination was Joseph Smith. "Joe Smith is not safe out of Nauvoo," trumpeted Sharp in the *Warsaw Signal*. "We would not be surprised to hear of his death by violent means in a short time."[132] To Joseph, such mobocratic threats were appalling. On June 18, 1844, in his last speech to the Nauvoo Legion, Joseph said, "I will never tamely submit to the dominion of cursed mobocracy."[133]

Why did Joseph Smith go to Carthage in June 1844?

About two o'clock in the morning of June 23, Joseph and his brother Hyrum were rowed across the Mississippi River from Nauvoo to Iowa. "There is no doubt [the mob element] will come [to Nauvoo] and search for us," Joseph said. "Let them search; they will not harm" the Mormon people.[134] Ill-advised friends in Iowa believed Latter-day Saints in Nauvoo would be harmed if Joseph and Hyrum did not return to Nauvoo. They encouraged the Prophet to face an arraignment in Carthage on the trumped-up charge of riot. With resignation Joseph said, "If my life is of no value to my friends it is of none to myself . . . *I am going like a lamb to the slaughter, but I am calm as a summer's morning. I have a conscience void of offense toward God and toward all men. If they take my life I shall die an innocent man, and my blood shall cry from the ground for vengeance, and it shall be said of me 'He was murdered in cold blood!'*"[135]

What happened in Carthage on June 27, 1844?

Accusations of riot stemming from the *Nauvoo Expositor* were turned to treason in Carthage. The militants in town unabashedly declared that the Smith brothers, Joseph and Hyrum, would not leave Carthage: "*There was nothing against these* men; *the law could not reach them but powder and ball would,* and they should not go out of Carthage alive."[136] A mob loitered outside the Carthage Jail, where Joseph and Hyrum were imprisoned. The mob sang: "Where now is the Prophet Joseph? Safe in Carthage jail!"[137] Even the governor of Illinois, Thomas Ford, joined the conspirators, mobbers, and militia in abetting the deaths of Joseph and Hyrum. A letter written to Emma reveals the sorrowful mood of the Prophet as he contemplated his death: "I am very much resigned to my lot, knowing I am justified and have done the best that could be done. Give my love to the children and all my friends. . . . May God bless you all."[138]

As the day waned, Joseph and Hyrum and two members of the Quorum of the Twelve Apostles, John Taylor and Willard Richards, lingered in the east bedroom of the Carthage Jail. There, Taylor sang "A Poor Wayfaring Man of Grief," which seemed to harmonize with the ominous foreboding of near events:

> In pris'n I saw him next—condemned
> To meet a traitor's doom at morn;
> The tide of lying tongues I stemmed.
> And honored him 'mid shame and scorn.
>
> My friendship's utmost zeal to try,
> He asked, if I for him would die;
> The flesh was weak, my blood ran chill,
> But my free spirit cried, "I will!"[139]

What happened in the final moments of Joseph Smith's life?

Around five in the afternoon of June 27, 1844, Willard Richards saw a hundred or more men running around the jail. John Taylor described them as "an armed mob—painted black-—of from 150 to 200 persons."[140] They rushed the stairs and began shooting into the east bedroom. Despite initial attempts to protect themselves from mob violence, the men were no match for the disguised mobbers. Hyrum was the first to fall from an assassin's bullet. As he backed away from the door to the center of the room, one bullet pierced the upper panel of the door and struck him on the left side of the nose. As he was falling to the floor, he exclaimed, *I am a dead man!*"[141] Bending over the body of his lifeless brother, Joseph sobbed, "Oh dear, brother Hyrum!"[142] As Joseph moved toward the east bedroom window, two bullets hit him from the doorway, and two struck him from the outside. He fell from the window to the ground below and exclaimed, *O Lord my God!*"[143] The mob had finished its murderous plot and Joseph, the Prophet, lay dead outside of the jail. The workers of destruction left more than the corpses of two men. They left "a broad seal affixed to 'Mormonism' that cannot be rejected by any court on earth, . . . [and] truth of the everlasting gospel that all the world cannot impeach."[144] The senseless brutality of the mob bequeathed crowns to the two martyrs.

How did Mormons react to the death of Joseph and Hyrum Smith?

Although thousands viewed the remains of the martyrs, their widows (Emma Smith and Mary Fielding Smith) were among the first to see them. "Yea I witnessed their tears, and groans, which was enough to rent the heart of an adamant," wrote Vilate Kimball. "Every brother and sister that witnessed the scene felt deeply to sympathize with them."[145] Poetess Eliza R. Snow wrote of their grief:

> All hearts with sorrow bleed, and every eye
> Is bath'd in tears—each bosom heaves a sigh—

Heartbroken widows' agonizing groans
Are mingled with the helpless orphans' moans![146]

John Taylor penned, "I felt a dull, lonely, sickening sensation at the news [of their deaths]. When I reflected that our noble chieftain, the Prophet of the living God, had fallen, and that I had seen his brother in the cold embrace of death, it seemed as though there was a void or vacuum in the great field of human existence to me, and a dark gloomy chasm in the kingdom, and that we were left alone."[147] Newel Knight lamented, "O how I loved those men, and rejoiced under their teachings! It seems as if all is gone, and as if my heart strings will break, and were it not for my beloved wife and dear children I feel as if I have nothing to live for."[148]

Did the death of the Smith brothers halt the spread of Mormonism?

"The death of the modern mahomet will seal the fate of Mormonism," announced a *New York Herald* editorial. "They cannot get another Joe Smith. . . . the 'latter day saints' have indeed come to the latter day."[149] Such a bold erase of the Church of Jesus Christ of Latter-day Saints was not the plan of God. Orson Hyde boldly announced, "I will prophesy that instead of the work dying, it will be like the mustard stock that was ripe, that a man undertook to throw out of his garden, and scattered seed all over it, and next year it was nothing but mustard. It will be so by shedding the blood of the Prophets—it will make ten saints where there is one now."[150]

Core Concepts of The Religious Teachings of Joseph Smith

What is the central belief of the Church of Jesus Christ of Latter-day Saints?

Joseph Smith said, "The fundamental principles of our religion are the testimony of the Apostles and Prophets, concerning Jesus Christ, that He died, was buried, and rose again the third day, and ascended into heaven; and all other things which pertain to our religion are only appendages to it."[151]

Do the Mormons have a creed?

In 1842 John Wentworth, editor of the *Chicago Tribune* newspaper, asked Joseph Smith for information about his church. In his reply, Joseph wrote thirteen statements, known as the Articles of Faith, which set forth fundamental doctrines of the Church of Jesus Christ of Latter-day Saints. These doctrines are as follows:

We believe in God the Eternal Father, and in His Son Jesus Christ, and in the Holy Ghost.

We believe that men will be punished for their own sins, and not for Adam's transgression.

We believe that through the atonement of Christ all mankind may be saved by obedience to the laws and ordinances of the Gospel.

We believe that the first principles and ordinances of the Gospel are: (1) Faith in the Lord Jesus Christ; (2) Repentance;

(3) Baptism by immersion for the remission of sins; (4) Laying on of hands for the gift of the Holy Ghost.

We believe that a man must be called of God by prophecy and by the laying on of hands, by those who are in authority, to preach the Gospel and administer in the ordinances thereof.

We believe in the same organization that existed in the primitive Church, viz: apostles, prophets, pastors, teachers, evangelists, etc.

We believe in the gift of tongues, prophecy, revelation, visions, healing, interpretation of tongues, etc.

We believe the Bible to be the word of God, as far as it is translated correctly; we also believe the Book of Mormon to be the word of God.

We believe all that God has revealed, all that He does now reveal, and we believe that He will yet reveal many great and important things pertaining to the kingdom of God.

We believe in the literal gathering of Israel and in the restoration of the Ten Tribes; that Zion will be built upon this [the American] continent; that Christ will reign personally upon the earth; and that the earth will be renewed and receive its paradisiacal glory.

We claim the privilege of worshiping Almighty God according to the dictates of our own conscience, and allow all men the same privilege, let them worship how, where, or what they may.

We believe in being subject to kings, presidents, rulers, and magistrates, in obeying, honoring, and sustaining the law.

We believe in being honest, true, chaste, benevolent, virtuous, and in doing good to *all men*; indeed we may say that we follow the admonition of Paul, We believe all things, we hope all things, we have endured many things, and hope to be able to endure all things. If there is anything virtuous, lovely, or of good report, or praiseworthy, we seek after these things.[152]

What did Joseph Smith teach about the Plan of Salvation—the purpose of life?

On October 9, 1843, in a discourse given in Nauvoo, Joseph taught, "The great plan of salvation is a theme which ought to occupy our strict attention, and be regarded as one of heaven's best gifts to mankind. All men know that they must die. And it is important that we should understand the reasons and causes of our exposure to the vicissitudes of life and of death, and the designs and purposes of God in our coming into the world, our sufferings here, and our departure hence. What is the object of our coming into existence, then dying and falling away, to be here no more? It is but reasonable to suppose that God would reveal something in reference to the matter, and it is a subject we ought to study more than any other. We ought to study it day and night, for the world is ignorant in reference to their true condition and relation [to God]."[153]

Did Joseph Smith believe the Bible was scripture?

Joseph said, "Notwithstanding the corruptions and abominations of the times, and the evil spirit manifested towards us on account of our belief in the Book of Mormon, at many places and among various persons, yet the Lord continued His watchful care and loving kindness to us day by day; and we made it a rule wherever there was an opportunity, to read a chapter in the Bible, and pray; and these seasons of worship gave us great consolation."[154] He added, "See God's own handwriting in the sacred volume: and he who reads it oftenest will like it best, and he who is acquainted with it, will know the hand wherever he can see it; and when once discovered, it will not only receive an acknowledgment, but an obedience to all its heavenly precepts."[155]

Did Joseph Smith teach the ten commandments?

Joseph taught, "Be virtuous and pure; be men of integrity

and truth; keep the commandments of God; and then you will be able more perfectly to understand the difference between right and wrong—between the things of God and the things of men; and your path will be like that of the just, which shineth brighter and brighter unto the perfect day."[156]

What were Joseph Smith's views on other religions?

On July 9, 1843, in a discourse given in Nauvoo, Joseph said, "The Saints can testify whether I am willing to lay down my life for my brethren. If it has been demonstrated that I have been willing to die for a 'Mormon,' I am bold to declare before Heaven that I am just as ready to die in defending the rights of a Presbyterian, a Baptist, or a good many of any other denomination; for the same principle which would trample upon the rights of the Latter-day Saints would trample upon the rights of the Roman Catholics, or of any other denomination who may be unpopular and too weak to defend themselves."[157] In a letter to Edward Partridge and the Church, written on March 20, 1839 from Liberty Jail, Joseph penned, "We ought always to be aware of those prejudices which sometimes so strangely present themselves, and are so congenial to human nature, against our friends, neighbors, and brethren of the world, who choose to differ from us in opinion and in matters of faith. Our religion is between us and our God. Their religion is between them and their God."[158]

What did Joseph Smith say about the need for a restoration?

On January 6, 1842, in Nauvoo, Joseph said, "Truly this is a day long to be remembered by the Saints of the last days,—a day in which the God of heaven has begun to restore the ancient order of His kingdom unto His servants and His people—a day in which all things are concurring to bring about the completion of the fullness of the Gospel, a fullness of the dispensation of dispensations, even the fullness of times; a day in which God has begun to make manifest and set in order in His Church those things which have been, and those things which the ancient prophets and wise men desired to see but died without beholding them; a day in which those things begin to be made manifest, which have been hid from before the foundation of the world, and which Jehovah has promised should be made known in His own due time unto His servants, to prepare the earth for the return of His glory, even a celestial glory, and a kingdom of Priests and kings to God and the Lamb, forever, on Mount Zion."[159]

What did Joseph Smith teach about the godhead?

On June 11, 1843, in a discourse given in Nauvoo, Joseph taught, "I have always declared God to be a distinct personage, Jesus Christ a separated and distinct personage from God the Father, and that the Holy Ghost was a distinct personage and a Spirit; and these three constitute three distinct personages and three Gods."[160] On April 7, 1844, in a discourse given at the funeral of King Follett, Joseph explained, "God himself was once as we are now, and is an exalted man, and sits enthroned in yonder heavens! That is the great secret. If the veil were rent today, and the great God who holds the world in its orbit, and who upholds all worlds and all things by His power, was to make himself visible,—I say, if you were to see him today, you would see him like a man in form—like yourselves in all the person, image, and very form as a man; for Adam was created in the very fashion, image and likeness of God, and received instruction from, and walked, talked and conversed with Him, as one man talks and communes with another. . . . It is the first principle of the gospel to know for a certainty the character of God, and to know that we may converse with Him as one man converses with another."[161]

What did Joseph Smith teach about Jesus Christ?

On July 23, 1843, in a discourse given in Nauvoo, Joseph said: "Christ was the head of the Church, the chief corner stone, the spiritual rock upon which the church was built, and the gates of hell shall not prevail against it. He built up the Kingdom, chose Apostles, and ordained them to the Melchizedek Priesthood, giving them power to administer in the ordinances of the Gospel. John was a priest after the order of Aaron before Christ."[162] Joseph added, "I am a lover of the cause of Christ and of virtue, chastity and an upright steady course of conduct and a holy walk. I believe in living a virtuous, upright, and holy life before God, and feel it my duty to persuade all men in my power to do the same, that they may cease to do evil and learn to do well, and break off their sins by righteousness."[163]

Did Joseph Smith teach that Jesus lived a perfect life?

On May 16, 1841, in a discourse given in Nauvoo, Joseph said, "None ever were perfect but Jesus; and why was He perfect? Because He was the Son of God, and had the fullness of the Spirit, and greater power than any man."[164] On November 23, 1833, in a letter to the brethren at Geneseo, New York, Joseph wrote, "When we reflect upon the holiness and perfections of our great Master, who has opened a way whereby we may come unto him, even by the sacrifice of himself, our hearts melt within us for his condescension. And when we reflect also, that he has called us to be perfect in all things, that we may be prepared to meet him in peace when he comes in his glory and with all the holy angels, we feel to exhort our brethren with boldness, to be humble and prayerful, to walk indeed as children of the light and of the day, that they may have grace to withstand every temptation, and to overcome every evil in the worthy name of our Lord Jesus Christ."[165]

What did Joseph Smith teach about the Holy Ghost?

Joseph said, "We believe that the holy men of old spake as they were moved by the Holy Ghost, and that holy men in these days speak by the same principle; we believe in its being a comforter and a witness bearer, that it brings things past to our remembrance, leads us into all truth, and shows us of things to come; we believe that 'no man can know that Jesus is the Christ, but by the Holy Ghost.'"[166]

Did Joseph Smith believe that man is in the image of God?

On July 9, 1843, in a discourse given in Nauvoo, Joseph said, "After God had created the heavens and the earth, he came down and on the sixth day said, let us make man in our own image. In whose image? In the image of the Gods created they them, male and female, innocent, harmless, and spotless, bearing the same character and the same image as the Gods. And when man fell he did not lose his image, but his character still retained the image of his maker, Christ, who is the image of man and is also the express image of his Father's person. . . . Through the atonement of Christ and the resurrection and obedience to the gospel, we shall again be conformed to the image of his Son, Jesus Christ; then we shall have attained to the image, glory, and character of God."[167]

How did Joseph Smith define faith?

On March 20, 1842, in a discourse given in Nauvoo, Joseph said, "There is no other way beneath the heavens whereby God hath ordained for man to come to Him to be saved, and enter into the kingdom of God, except faith in Jesus Christ, repentance, and baptism for the remission of sins, and any other course is in vain."[168] He added, "Faith, then, is the first great governing principle which has power, dominion, and authority over all things; by it they exist, by it they are upheld, by it they are changed, or by it they remain, agreeable to the will of God. Without it there is no power, and without power there could be no creation nor existence!"[169] Joseph added, "Without faith it is impossible to please God. If it should be asked—Why is it impossible to please God without faith? The answer would be—Because without faith it is impossible for men to be saved, and as God desires the salvation of men, he must, of course, desire that they should have faith; and he could not be pleased unless they had, or else he could be pleased with their destruction."[170]

What did Joseph Smith teach about repentance?

On January 11, 1833, in a letter to William W. Phelps, Joseph penned, "They who will not hear [the Lord's] voice, must expect to feel His wrath. Let me say unto you, seek to purify yourselves, and also all the inhabitants of Zion, lest the Lord's anger be kindled to fierceness. Repent, repent, is the voice of God to Zion; and strange as it may appear, yet it is true, mankind will persist in self-justification until all their iniquity is exposed, and their character past being redeemed, and that which is treasured up in their hearts be exposed to the gaze of mankind. I say to you (and what I say to you I say to all), hear the warning voice of God."[171] On June 27, 1839, in a discourse given in Commerce, Joseph said, "Repentance is a thing that cannot be trifled with every day. Daily transgression and daily repentance is not that which is pleasing in the sight of God."[172] On March 20, 1842, in a discourse given in Nauvoo, Joseph taught, "We should take warning and not wait for the death-bed to repent; as we see the infant taken away by death, so may the youth and middle aged, as well as the infant be suddenly called into eternity. Let this, then, prove as a warning to all not to procrastinate repentance, or wait till a death-bed, for it is the will of God that man should repent and serve Him in health, and in the strength and power of his mind, in order to secure His blessing, and not wait until he is called to die."[173]

Why did Joseph Smith believe baptism was essential?

On March 20, 1842, in a discourse given in Nauvoo, Joseph said, "Baptism is a sign to God, to angels, and to heaven that we do the will of God, and there is no other way beneath the heavens whereby God hath ordained for man to come to Him to be saved, and enter into the kingdom of God, except faith in Jesus Christ, repentance, and baptism for the remission of sins, and any other course is in vain."[174] On September 1, 1842, acting as editor of the *Times and Seasons*, Joseph wrote, "Upon looking over the sacred pages of the Bible, searching into the prophets and sayings of the apostles, we find no subject so nearly connected with salvation, as that of baptism. . . . It may not be amiss to introduce the commissions and commands of Jesus himself on the subject.—He said to the twelve, or rather eleven at the time: Go ye therefore, and teach all nations, baptizing them in the name of the Father, and of the Son, and of the Holy Ghost: teaching them to observe all things whatsoever I have commanded you: Thus it is recorded by Matthew. In Mark we have these important words: Go ye into all the world, and preach the gospel to every creature. He that believeth and is baptized shall be saved, and he that believeth not shall be damned."[175]

Why was Joseph Smith opposed to infant baptism?

On March 20, 1842, in a discourse given in Nauvoo, Joseph explained, "The doctrine of baptizing children, or sprinkling them, or they must welter in hell, is a doctrine not true, not supported in Holy Writ, and is not consistent with the character of God. All children are redeemed by the blood of

Jesus Christ, and the moment that children leave this world, they are taken to the bosom of Abraham."[176]

Did Joseph Smith distinguish between the Holy Ghost and the gift of the Holy Ghost?

On March 20, 1842, in a discourse given in Nauvoo, Joseph said, "Cornelius received the Holy Ghost before he was baptized, which was the convincing power of God unto him of the truth of the Gospel, but he could not receive the gift of the Holy Ghost until after he was baptized. Had he not taken this sign or ordinance upon him, the Holy Ghost which convinced him of the truth of God, would have left him."[177]

What is the gift of the Holy Ghost?

On March 22, 1839, in a letter to Isaac Galland from Liberty Jail, Joseph Smith penned, "We believe that we have a right to revelations, visions, and dreams from God, our heavenly Father; and light and intelligence, through the gift of the Holy Ghost, in the name of Jesus Christ, on all subjects pertaining to our spiritual welfare; if it so be that we keep his commandments, so as to render ourselves worthy in his sight."[178] On July 9, 1843, in a discourse given in Nauvoo, Joseph espoused, "I further believe in the gift of the Holy Ghost by the laying on of hands—evidence by Peter's preaching on the day of Pentecost. You might as well baptize a bag of sand as a man, if not done in view of the remission of sins and getting of the Holy Ghost. Baptism by water is but half a baptism, and is good for nothing without the other half—that is, the baptism of the Holy Ghost. The Savior says, 'Except a man be born of water and of the Spirit, he cannot enter into the kingdom of God.'"[179]

What did Joseph Smith teach about prayer?

Joseph taught, "Seek to know God in your closets, call

upon him in the fields. Follow the directions of the Book of Mormon, and pray over, and for your families, your cattle, your flocks, your herds, your corn, and all things that you possess; ask the blessing of God upon all your labors, and everything that you engage in."[180] Joseph further taught, "Slack not your duties in your families, but call upon God for his blessings upon you, and your families—upon your flocks and herds, and all that pertains to you—that you may have peace and prosperity—and while you are doing this, 'pray for the peace of Zion, for they shall prosper that love her.'"[181]

Why did Joseph Smith stress the importance of prayer?

On March 20, 1839, in a letter to Edward Partridge and the Church written in Liberty Jail, Joseph said, "The things of God are of deep import; and time, and experiences, and careful and ponderous and solemn thoughts can only find them out. Thy mind, O man! If thou wilt lead a soul unto salvation, must stretch as high as the utmost heavens, and search into and contemplate the darkest abyss, and the broad expanse of eternity—thou must commune with God. How much more dignified and noble are the thoughts of God, than the vain imaginations of the human heart! None but fools will trifle with the souls of men."[182]

How do people learn religious truths?

On April 7, 1844, at the funeral of King Follett, Joseph taught, "When you climb up a ladder, you must begin at the bottom, and ascend step by step, until you arrive at the top; and so it is with the principles of the gospel—you must begin with the first, and go on until you learn all the principles of exaltation. But it will be a great while after you have passed through the veil before you will have learned them. It is not all to be comprehended in this world; it will be a great work to learn our salvation and exaltation even beyond the grave."[183]

What is the spirit of revelation?

On June 27, 1839, in a discourse given in Commerce, Joseph Smith said, "A person may profit by noticing the first intimation of the spirit of revelations; for instance, when you feel pure intelligence flowing into you, it may give you sudden strokes of ideas, so that by noticing it, you may find it fulfilled the same day or soon; (i.e.) Those things that were presented unto your minds by the Spirit of God, will come to pass; and thus by learning the Spirit of God and understanding it, you may grow into the principle of revelation, until you become perfect in Christ Jesus."[184] Joseph added, "Without [revelation] we can neither know nor understand anything of God, or the devil; and however unwilling the world may be to acknowledge this principle, it is evident from the multifarious creeds and notions concerning this matter that they understand nothing of this principle, and it is equally as plan that without a divine communication they must remain in ignorance."[185]

What is the Mormon belief of authority to act in the name of God?

On March 22, 1839, in a letter to Isaac Galland written from Liberty Jail, Joseph Smith penned, "We believe that no man can administer salvation through the gospel, to the souls of men, in the name of Jesus Christ, except he is authorized from God, by revelation, or by being ordained by someone whom God hath sent by revelation."[186]

Do Latter-day Saints trace priesthood authority to ancient prophets?

In July of 1839, in a discourse given in Commerce, Joseph

said, "The Priesthood was first given to Adam; he obtained the First Presidency, and held the keys of it from generation to generation. He obtained it in the Creation, before the world was formed. He had dominion given him over every living creature. He is Michael the Archangel, spoken of in the Scriptures. Then to Noah, who is Gabriel; he stands next in authority to Adam in the Priesthood; he was called of God to this office, and was the father of all living in his day, and to him was given the dominion. These men held keys first on earth, and then in heaven. The priesthood is an everlasting principle, and existed with God from eternity, and will to eternity, without beginning of days or end of years. The keys have to be brought from heaven whenever the Gospel is sent."[187]

What is the Melchizedek priesthood?

Joseph Smith said, "The power and authority of the higher, or Melchizedek Priesthood, is to hold the keys of all the spiritual blessings of the church—to have the privilege of receiving the mysteries of the kingdom of heaven, to have the heavens opened unto them, to commune with the general assembly and church of the Firstborn, and to enjoy the communion and presence of God the Father, and Jesus the mediator of the new covenant."[188]

What is the laying on of hands?

On March 20, 1842, in a discourse given in Nauvoo, Joseph Smith said, "The laying on of hands is the sign or way marked out by James, and the custom of the ancient Saints as ordered by the Lord, and we cannot obtain the blessing by pursuing any other course except the way marked out by the Lord."[189]

Did Joseph Smith believe in the creation?

Joseph said, "The heavens declare the glory of a God, and

the firmament showeth His handiwork; and a moment's reflection is sufficient to teach every man of common intelligence, that all these are not the mere production of *chance*, nor could they be supported by any power less than an Almighty hand."[190] On March 20, 1842, in a discourse given in Nauvoo, Joseph said, "God has made certain decrees which are fixed and immovable; for instance,—God set the sun, the moon, and the stars in the heavens, and gave them their laws, conditions and bounds, which they cannot pass, except by His commandments, they all move in perfect harmony in their sphere and order, and are as lights, wonders and signs unto us. The sea also has its bounds which it cannot pass. . . . It is a decree of the Lord that every tree, plant, and herb bearing seed should bring forth of its kind, and cannot come forth after any other law or principle."[191]

Did Joseph Smith teach of foreordination?

Joseph explained, "All persons are entitled to their agency, for God has so ordained it. He has constituted mankind moral agents, and given them power to choose good or evil; to seek after that which is good, by pursuing the pathway of holiness in this life, which brings peace of mind, and joy in the Holy Ghost here, and a fulness of joy and happiness at His right hand hereafter; or to pursue an evil course, going on in sin and rebellion against God, thereby bringing condemnation to their souls in this world, and an eternal loss in the world to come."[192]

Do Mormons believe the devil can force people to make bad choices?

In a November 1839 letter from Joseph Smith and his counselors in the First Presidency, it was said, "All persons are entitled to their agency, for God has so ordained it. He has constituted mankind moral agents, and given them power to choose good or evil; to seek after that which is good, by pursuing the pathway of holiness in this life, which brings peace of mind, and joy in the Holy Ghost here, and a fulness of joy and happiness at His right hand hereafter; or to pursue an evil course, going on in sin and rebellion against God, thereby bringing condemnation to their souls in this world, and an eternal loss in the world to come."[193] On January 5, 1841, in a discourse given in Nauvoo, Joseph said, "The devil has no power over us only as we permit him."[194]

Did Joseph Smith recognize that false prophets walked the earth?

Joseph taught, "The world always mistook false prophets for true ones, and those that were sent of God, they considered to be false prophets, and hence they killed, stoned, punished and imprisoned the true prophets, and these had to hide themselves 'in deserts and dens, and caves of the earth,' and though the most honorable men of the earth, they banished them from their society as vagabonds, whilst they cherished, honored and supported knaves, vagabonds, hypocrites, impostors, and the basest of men."[195]

Did Joseph Smith write of the importance of obeying civil law?

On June 22, 1844, Joseph wrote to Thomas Ford, governor of Illinois, "Our troubles are invariably brought upon us by falsehood and misrepresentation by designing men; we have ever held ourselves amenable to the law, and for myself, Sir, I am every ready to conform to and support the laws and constitution even at the expense of my life. I have never in the least offered any resistance to law, or lawful process, which is a fact well known to the public."[196]

Why did Joseph Smith think temple ordinances were so important?

On June 11, 1843, in a discourse given in Nauvoo, Joseph said, "All men who become heirs of God and joint-heirs with Jesus Christ will have to receive the fulness of the ordinances of his kingdom; and those who will not receive all the ordinances will come short of the fullness of that glory."[197] On January 21, 1844, in a discourse given in Nauvoo, Joseph said, "The question is frequently asked 'Can we not be saved without going through with all those ordinances, etc.?' I would answer, No, not the fullness of salvation. Jesus said, 'There are many mansions in my Father's house, and I will go and prepare a place for you.'"[198]

What is the doctrine of baptism for the dead?

On April 7, 1844, at the funeral of King Follett, Joseph said, "What promises are made in relation to the subject of the salvation of the dead? and what kind of characters are those who can be saved, although their bodies are moldering and decaying in the grave? When His commandments teach us, it is in view of eternity; for we are looked upon by God as though we were in eternity; God dwells in eternity, and does not view things as we do. The greatest responsibility in this world that God has laid upon us is to seek after our dead. The apostle [Peter] says,"They without us cannot be made perfect;" for it is necessary that the sealing power should be in our hands to seal our children and our dead for the fulness of the dispensation of times—a dispensation to meet the promises made by Jesus Christ before the foundation of the world for the salvation of man."[199] In the same discourse, Joseph said, "Every man who wishes to save his father, mother, brothers, sisters, and friends, must go through all the ordinances for each one of them separately, the same as for himself, from baptism to ordination, washings and anointings, and receive all the keys and powers of the Priesthood, the same as for himself."[200]

What did Joseph Smith teach about the resurrection?

On April 16, 1843, in a discourse given in Nauvoo, Joseph taught, "God has revealed His Son from the heavens and the doctrine of the resurrection also; and we have a knowledge that those we bury here God will bring up again, clothed upon and quickened by the Spirit of the great God; and what mattereth it whether we lay them down, or we lay down with them, when we can keep them no longer? Let these truths sink down in our hearts, that we may even here begin to enjoy that which shall be in full hereafter."[201] On June 11, 1843, in a discourse given in Nauvoo, Joseph said, "'But,' says one, 'I believe in one universal heaven and hell, where all go, and are all alike, and equally miserable or equally happy.' What! where all are huddled together—the honorable, virtuous, and murderers, and whoremongers, when it is written that they shall be judged according to the deeds done in the body. But St. Paul informs us of three glories and three heavens. He knew a man that was caught up to the third heavens . . . Jesus said unto His disciples, 'In my Father's house are many mansions, if it were not so, I would have told you. I go to prepare a place for you, and I will come and receive you to myself, that where I am ye may be also.'"[202] On May 12, 1844, in another discourse given in Nauvoo, Joseph said, "'In my Father's house are many mansions.' It should be—'In my Father's kingdom are many kingdoms,' in order that ye may be heirs of God and joint-heirs with me. . . . There are mansions for those who obey a celestial law, and there are other mansions for those who come short of the law, every man in his own order."

What were Joseph Smith's teachings on the death of children?

On March 20, 1842, in a discourse given in Nauvoo, Joseph taught, "We have again the warning voice sounded in our midst, which shows the uncertainty of human life; and in my leisure moments I have meditated upon the subject, and asked the question, why it is that infants, innocent children, are taken away from us, especially those that seem to be the most intelligent and interesting. The strongest reasons that present themselves to my mind are these: This world is a very wicked world; and it . . . grows more wicked and corrupt. . . . The Lord takes many away, even in infancy, that they may escape the envy of man, and the sorrows and evils of this present world; they are too pure, too lovely, to live on earth; therefore, if rightly considered, instead of mourning we have reason to rejoice as they are delivered from evil, and we shall soon have them again."[203]

Will we have family relationships in heaven?

On April 16, 1843, in a discourse given in Nauvoo, Joseph Smith said, "If I have no expectation of seeing my father, mother, brothers, sisters and friends again, my heart would burst in a moment, and I should go down to my grave. The expectation of seeing my friends in the morning of the resurrection cheers my soul and makes me bear up against the evils of life. It is like their taking a long journey, and on their return we meet them with increased joy."[204] On April 7, 1844, at the funeral of King Follett, Joseph said, "I have a father, brothers, children, and friends who have gone to a world of spirits. They are only absent for a moment. They are in the spirit, and we shall soon meet again. The time will soon arrive when the trumpet shall sound. When we depart, we shall hail our mothers, fathers, friends, and all whom we love, who have fallen asleep in Jesus. There will be no fear of mobs, persecutions, or malicious lawsuits and arrests; but it will be an eternity of felicity."[205]

What are Joseph Smith's teachings on love?

On December 15, 1840, Joseph wrote to elders in Great

Britain, "Love is one of the chief characteristics of Deity, and ought to be manifested by those who aspire to be the sons of God. A man filled with the love of God, is not content with blessing his family alone, but ranges through the whole world, anxious to bless the whole human race."[206] On July 23, 1843, in a discourse given in Nauvoo, Joseph taught, "It is a time-honored adage that love begets love. Let us pour forth love— show forth love—show forth our kindness unto all mankind, and the Lord will reward us with everlasting increase; cast our bread upon the waters and we shall receive it after many days, increased to a hundredfold."[207] Joseph further said, "It is the duty which every Saint ought to render to his brethren freely—to always love them, and ever succor them. To be justified before God we must love one another: we must overcome evil; we must visit the fatherless and the widow in their affliction, and we must keep ourselves unspotted from the world; for such virtues flow from the great fountain of pure religion."[208]

What did Joseph Smith teach about charity?

Joseph taught, "Consider the state of the afflicted and try to alleviate their sufferings; let your bread feed the hungry, and your clothing cover the naked; let your liberality dry up the tear of the orphan, and cheer the disconsolate widow; let your prayers, and presence, and kindness, alleviate the pains of the distressed, and your liberality contribute to their necessities; do good unto all men, especially unto the household of faith, that you may be harmless and blameless, the sons of God without rebuke. Keep the commandments of God—all that he has given, does give, or will give, and a halo of glory will shine around your path; the poor will rise up and call you blessed; you will be honored and respected by all good men; and your path will be that of the just, which shineth brighter and brighter until the perfect day."[209] On April 28, 1842, in a discourse given in

Nauvoo, Joseph added, "'Though I speak with the tongues of men and angels, and have not charity, I am become as sounding brass, or a tinkling cymbal;' and said, don't be limited in your views with regard to your neighbor's virtue, but beware of self-righteousness, and be limited in the estimate of your own virtues, and not think yourselves more righteous than others; you must enlarge your souls towards each other, if you would do like Jesus, and carry your fellow-creatures to Abraham's bosom. He said he had manifested long-suffering, forbearance and patience towards the Church, and also to his enemies; and we must bear with each other's failings, as an indulgent parent bears with the foibles of his children. . . . As you increase in innocence and virtue, as you increase in goodness, let your hearts expand, let them be enlarged towards others; you must be long-suffering, and bear with the faults and errors of mankind. How precious are the souls of men!"[210]

What did Joseph Smith teach about the duty of a husband to his wife?

Joseph taught: "It is the duty of a husband to love, cherish, and nourish his wife, and cleave unto her and none else; he ought to honor her as himself, and he ought to regard her feelings with tenderness, for she is his flesh, and his bone, designed to be an help unto him, both in temporal, and spiritual things; one into whose bosom he can pour out all his complaints without reserve, who is willing (being designed) to take part of his burden, to soothe and encourage his feelings by her gentle voice."[211]

What does Joseph Smith say about the role of a father?

Joseph said: "It is the place of the man, to stand at the head of his family, to be lord of his own house, not to rule over his wife as a tyrant, neither as one who is fearful or jealous that his wife will get out of her place, and prevents him from exercising his authority. It is his duty to be a man of God (for a man of God is a man of wisdom) ready at all times to obtain from the scriptures, the revelations, and from on high, such instructions as are necessary for the edification, and salvation of his household."[212]

Did Joseph Smith have counsel for how wives should treat their husbands?

On April 28, 1842, in a discourse given in Nauvoo, Joseph counseled, "Teach women how to behave towards their husbands, to treat them with mildness and affection. When a man is borne down with trouble, when he is perplexed with care and difficulty, if he can meet a smile instead of an argument or a murmur—if he can meet with mildness, it will calm down his soul and soothe his feelings; when the mind is going to despair, it needs a solace of affection and kindness. . . .When you go home, never give a cross or unkind word to your husbands, but let kindness, charity and love crown your works henceforward."[213]

What did Joseph Smith teach about caring for the aged?

On December 18, 1835, in a letter to his brother William Smith, Joseph penned, "When we reflect with what care, and with what unremitting diligence our parents have striven to watch over us, and how many hours of sorrow and anxiety they have spent, over our cradles and bed-sides, in times of sickness, how careful we ought to be of their feelings in their old age! It cannot be a source of sweet reflection to us, to say or do anything that will bring their gray hairs down with sorrow to the grave."[214]

What is the expected reward of those who stand stead-fast through the storms of life?

On April 7, 1841, Joseph Smith and his counselors in the First Presidency, penned, "Stand fast, ye Saints of God, hold on a little while longer, and the storm of life will be past, and you will be rewarded by that God whose servants you are, and who will duly appreciate all your toils and afflictions for Christ's sake and the Gospel's. Your names will be handed down to posterity as Saints of God."[215]

With all the evil around, will righteousness triumph?

On January 1, 1836, Joseph Smith explained, "I know that the cloud will burst, and Satan's kingdom be laid in ruins, with all his black designs; and that the Saints will come forth like gold seven times tried in the fire, being made perfect through sufferings and temptations, and that the blessings of heaven and earth will be multiplied upon their heads; which may God grant for Christ's sake."[216]

What signs precede the Second Coming of Jesus Christ?

In July 1839, in a discourse given in Commerce, Joseph Smith said, "I will prophesy that the signs of the coming of the Son of Man are already commenced. One pestilence will desolate after another. We shall soon have war and bloodshed. The moon will be turned into blood. I testify of these things, and that the coming of the Son of Man is nigh, even at your doors. If our souls and our bodies are not looking forth for the coming of the Son of Man; and after we are dead, if we are not looking forth, we shall be among those who are calling for the rocks to fall upon them."[217] On April 6, 1843, in a discourse given in Nauvoo, Joseph added, "Judah must return, Jerusalem must be rebuilt, and the temple, and water come out from under the temple, and the waters of the Dead Sea be healed. It will take some time to rebuild the walls of the city and the temple, etc.; and all this must be done before the Son of Man will make His appearance. There will be wars and rumors of wars, signs in the heavens above and on the earth beneath, the sun turned into darkness and the moon to blood, earthquakes in divers places, the seas heaving beyond their bounds; then will appear one grand sign of the Son of Man in heaven. But what will the world do? They will say it is a planet, a comet, etc. But the Son of Man will come as the sign of the coming of the Son of Man, which will be as the light of the morning cometh out of the east."[218]

Comments by Contemporaries of Joseph Smith

Thousands of Latter-day Saints in the nineteenth-century resonated to Joseph Smith's declarations of prophetic revelation. Although contemporaries labeled them odd, if not ordinary folk, there was nothing ordinary about their willingness to follow Joseph from New York to Illinois. Their handwritten journal entries reveal an unusual saga of courage and unflinching faith at a time when religious intolerance was unchecked. Their courage to withstand cruel persecution and encroaching evil and their faith to look to God when all around them seemed to mock their convictions is an unparalleled story of religious commitment. As the world tossed with waves of uncertainty, their strength became a beacon to others searching for eternal truths. Their preserved statements of Joseph Smith help us better understand who he was and the impact he had upon his followers.

"My testimony of [Joseph Smith] is that he was a true Prophet of God, raised up in this last dispensation of the fulness of times, and that his sayings and teachings are true and faithful."

—*Thomas Cottam* [219]

"The more I heard his sayings and saw his doings the more I was convinced that he had of a truth seen God the Father and His Son Jesus Christ."

—*Daniel D. McArthur* [220]

"I feel like shouting hallelujah, all the time, when I think that I ever knew Joseph Smith, the Prophet whom the Lord raised up and ordained, and to whom He gave keys and power to build up the kingdom of God on earth."

—Brigham Young [221]

"He was a prophet of God, and he laid the foundation of the greatest work and dispensation that has ever been established on the earth."

—Wilford Woodruff [222]

"This summer [of 1841 in Nauvoo] I played my first game of ball with the Prophet. We took turns knocking and chasing the ball, and when the game was over the Prophet said, 'Brethren, hitch up your teams'; which we did, and we all drove to the woods. . . . There were 39 teams in the group and we gathered wood until our wagons were loaded . . . Afterwards, the Prophet sent the wagons out to different places of people who needed help; and he told them to cut the wood for the Saints who needed it."

—Mosiah Hancock [223]

"To him there were no strangers and by all he was known as the Prophet and a friend of humanity."

—Mercy Thompson [224]

"The love the saints had for him was inexpressible. They would willingly have laid down their lives for him. If he was to talk, every task would be laid aside that they might listen to his words."

—Mary Lambert [225]

"It was Joseph Smith who taught me how to prize the endearing relationships of father and mother, husband and wife; of brother and sister, son and daughter. It was from him that

I learned that the wife of my bosom might be secured to me for time and all eternity; and that the refined sympathies and affections which endeared us to each other emanated from the fountain of divine eternal love. It was from him that I learned that we might cultivate these affections, and grow and increase in the same to all eternity; while the result of our endless union would be an offspring as numerous as the stars of heaven, or the sands of the sea shore."

—*Parley P. Pratt* [226]

"Joseph Smith is a great man, a man of principle, a straight forward man; no saintish long-faced fellow, but quite the reverse. Indeed some stumble because he is such a straight forward, plain spoken cheerful man, but that makes me love him the more."

—*John Needham* [227]

"Truly I wish I was such a man."

—*William Clayton* [228]

"No amusements or games were as interesting to me as to hear [Joseph Smith] talk."

—*Alvah Alexander* [229]

"I have even known [Joseph Smith] to retain a congregation of willing and anxious listeners for many hours together, in the midst of cold or sunshine, rain or wind, while they were laughing at one moment and weeping the next."

—*Parley P. Pratt* [230]

"The Lord told Joseph that He would prove him, whether he would abide in His covenant or not, even unto death. He did prove him; and although [Joseph] had the whole world to contend against and the treachery of false friends to withstand, although his whole life was a scene of trouble and anxiety and care, yet, in all his afflictions, his imprisonments, the mobbings and ill treatment he passed through he was ever true to his God."

—*Wilford Woodruff* [231]

"I have listened to the Prophet Joseph in public, and in private, in sunshine and shower—as many others have done as he taught from the stand—at my own house, and at his house, I have been familiar with him from the time he escaped from prison in Missouri in 1839 until his martyrdom in 1844, and do know that no man could explain the scriptures—throw them wide open to view, so plain that none could misunderstand their meaning—except he had been taught of God."

—*Wandle Mace* [232]

"In doctrine Mr. Smith is eminently scriptural. I have never known him to deny or depreciate a single truth of the Old and New Testaments; but I have always known him to explain and defend them in a masterly manner."

—*Orson Spencer* [233]

"I do not think that a man lives on the earth that knew [Joseph Smith] any better than I did; and I am bold to say that, Jesus Christ excepted, no better man ever lived or does live upon this earth. I am his witness."

—*Brigham Young* [234]

"In 1838 Joseph and some of the young men were playing various out-door games, among which was a game of ball. By and by they began to get weary. He saw it, and calling them together he said: 'Let us build a log cabin.' So, off they went, Joseph and the young men, to build a log cabin for a widow woman. Such was Joseph's way, always assisting in whatever he could."

—*Edwin Holden* [235]

"Some years ago, in Nauvoo, a gentleman in my hearing, a member of the Legislature, asked Joseph Smith how it was that he was enabled to govern so many people, and to preserve such perfect order; remarking at the same time that it was impossible for them to do it anywhere else. Mr. Smith remarked that it was very easy to do that. 'How?' responded the gentleman; 'to us it is very difficult.' Mr. Smith replied, 'I teach them correct principles, and they govern themselves.'"

—John Taylor [236]

"The Prophet Joseph Smith . . . told us that the Lord had revealed to him a principle whereby we could go forth and redeem our dead. It was like a shaft of light from the throne of God to our hearts. It opened a field wide as eternity to our minds."

—Wilford Woodruff [237]

"When the Spirit prompted him that his life's work was drawing to a close, and when he saw that his earthly days might be ended before the completion of the temple—he called a chosen few, and conferred upon them the ordinances of the holy endowments, so that the divine treasures of his mind might not perish from the world with his death."

—Franklin D. Richards [238]

"I have never saw anything like it on the earth, I could not take my eyes off him."

—Mary Elizabeth Rollins [239]

"The Prophet's voice was like the thunders of heaven, yet his language meek and his instructions edified much. There was a power and majesty that attended his words and preaching that we never beheld in any man before."

—Joseph L. Robinson [240]

"I saw the Prophet Joseph for the first time in May of [1843]. He was with about a dozen others on the stand in a meeting. I knew him as soon as I saw him. Although I was young I knew him to be a man of God. A few days after this I was at Joseph's house; he was there, and several men were sitting on the fence. Joseph came out and spoke to us all. Pretty soon a man came up and said that a poor brother who lived out some distance from town had had his house burned down the night before. Nearly all of the men said they felt sorry for the man. Joseph put his hand in his pocket, took out five dollars and said, 'I feel sorry for this brother to the amount of five dollars; how much do you all feel sorry?'"

—*Andrew J. Workman* [241]

"[Joseph] would unravel the scriptures and explain doctrine as no other man could. What had been mystery he made so plain it was no longer mystery."

—*Wandle Mace* [242]

"Truly God is with [Joseph Smith] and is making him mighty in wisdom and knowledge. And I am convinced for myself that none of the prophets, seers, or revelators of the earth have ever accomplished a greater work than will be accomplished in the last days through the mercy of God by Joseph the Seer."

—*Wilford Woodruff* [243]

"It was decreed in the counsels of eternity, long before the foundations of the earth were laid, that [Joseph Smith] should be the man, in the last dispensation of this world, to bring forth the word of God to the people, and receive the fullness of the keys and power of the Priesthood of the Son of God."

—*Brigham Young* [244]

"You knew he was a true prophet of God because you could not be in his presence without feeling the influence and Spirit of God, which seemed to flow from him almost as heat does from a stove. You could not see it, but you felt it."

—*William Henrie* [245]

"When I reflected that our noble chieftain, the Prophet of the living God, had fallen, and that I had seen his brother in the cold embrace of death, it seemed as though there was a void or vacuum in the great field of human existence to me, and a dark and gloomy chasm in the kingdom, and that we were left alone. Oh, how lonely was that feeling! How cold, barren and desolate! In the midst of difficulties he was always the first in motion; in critical positions his counsel was always sought. As our Prophet, he approached our God, and obtained for us his will; but now our Prophet, our counselor, our general, our leader, was gone."

—John Taylor [246]

"While visiting with brother Joseph in Philadelphia [in 1839], a very large church was opened for him to preach in, and about three thousand people assembled to hear him. Brother Rigdon spoke first, and dwelt on the Gospel, illustrating his doctrine by the Bible. When he was through, brother Joseph arose like a lion about to roar; and being full of the Holy Ghost, spoke in great power, bearing testimony of the visions he had seen, the ministering of angels which he had enjoyed; and how he had found the plates of the Book of Mormon, and translated them by the gift and power of God. He commenced by saying: 'If nobody else had the courage to testify of so glorious a message from Heaven, and of the finding of so glorious a record, he felt to do it in justice to the people, and leave the event with God.'"

—Parley P. Pratt [247]

"The Prophet Joseph and cousin Hyrum, his brother, visited us. We were all sick but Mother with the fever and ague and Father was out of his head the greatest part of the time. Joseph took the shoes from his feet when he saw our destitute condition and put them on Father's feet, as he was barefoot. [Joseph Smith] rode home without any himself. He sent and took Father home to his house and saved his life and supplied us with many [things] so we recovered."

—John Lyman Smith [248]

"The people loved to hear him, because he was full of revelation."

—Lorenzo Snow [249]

"I sat and listened to his preaching at the stand in Nauvoo a great many times when I have been completely carried away with his indescribable eloquence—power of expression—speaking as I have never heard any other man speak—I have heard him prophesy many things that have already come to pass."

—Howard Coray [250]

"He is a man that you could not help liking as a man, setting aside the religious prejudice which the world has raised against him. He is one of the warmest patriots and friends to his country and laws that you ever heard speak on the subject."

—George W. Taggart [251]

"As a Seer and Revelator he was fearless and outspoken, yet humble, never considering that he was more than the mouthpiece through whom God spoke."

—Jane S. Richards [252]

"[Joseph] told me I should never get discouraged, whatever difficulties might surround me. If I were sunk into the lowest pit of Nova Scotia and all the Rocky Mountains piled on top of me I ought not to be discouraged, but hang on, exercise faith, and keep up good courage, and I should come out on top of the heap."

—George A. Smith [253]

"I heard Joseph say to some elders going on missions, 'Make short prayers and short sermons, and let mysteries alone. Preach nothing but repentance and baptism for the remission of sins, for that was all John the Baptist preached.'"

—*Henry W. Bigler* [254]

"I have heard his voice. I have seen his face literally shine, illuminated from within by the effulgence of the Holy Spirit, and I testify to you that he was in very deed, a prophet of God."

—*William H. Maughan* [255]

"I heard him preach a number of times and saw him in and around the city, giving counsel, and I always believed in him from my first seeing him until his death, that he was the leader of this dispensation and God Almighty's prophet."

—*William C. Staines* [256]

"As a religious teacher, as well as a man, he is greatly beloved by this people."

—*John M. Bernhisel* [257]

"I felt when in his presence that he could read me through and through. I know he was all that he claimed to be."

—*Jesse N. Smith* [258]

"It is by no means improbable that some future textbook for the use of generations yet unborn, will contain a question something like this: What historical American of the nineteenth century has exerted the most powerful influence upon the destinies of his countrymen? And it is by no means impossible that the answer to the interrogatory may be thus written: Joseph Smith, the Mormon Prophet."

—*Josiah Quincy, a former mayor of Boston* [259]

Joseph Smith was a Prophet of God

Millions throughout the world embrace the word of God as taught by Joseph Smith. In song, they praise his memory:

Praise to the man who communed with Jehovah!
Jesus anointed that Prophet and Seer.
Blessed to open the last dispensation,
Kings shall extol him, and nations revere.

Praise to his mem'ry, he died as a martyr;
Honored and blest be his ever great name!
Long shall his blood, which was shed by assassins,
Plead unto heav'n while the earth lauds his fame.[260]

As one who writes of his memory, I declare that he was the "choice seer" whom the Lord raised up to bring forth the word of God. Revelations, translations, covenants, and eternal truths were the continuum of his life's labor for he held "the keys of this Last Dispensation, and will for ever hold them, both in time and eternity."[261] "The Lord Almighty sealed upon [his] head every Priesthood, every key, every power, every principle that belongs to the last dispensation of the fullness of times, and to the building up of the kingdom of God."[262] He was a prophet of God. The Church of Jesus Christ of Latter-day Saints is Christ's church restored. To this I testify.

Notes

1. Joseph Smith—History 1:25.
2. "Church Book of the Reformed Church of Christ in Fayette Township, Seneca County in State of New York, 1833," as cited in Larry C. Porter, "Organizational Origins of the Church of Jesus Christ, 6 April 1830," *Regional Studies in Latter-day Saint Church History: New York* eds. Larry C. Porter, Milton V. Backman Jr., Susan Easton Black (Provo, Utah: Department of Church History and Doctrine, Brigham Young University, 1992), 161.
3. Joseph Smith Jr., *History of the Church of Jesus Christ of Latter-day Saints* 7 vols. (Salt Lake City: Deseret Book, 1932–1951), 1:51, 81.
4. Quoted from a statement by John D. Spring, M.D., Nashau, New Hampshire, May 27, 1970, as cited in Larry C. Porter, "A Study of the Origins of the Church of Jesus Christ of Latter-day Saints in the States of New York and Pennsylvania, 1816–1831" (Ph.D. diss.), Brigham Young University, 1971, 19, 23n.
5. Lucy Mack Smith, *Biographical Sketches—Joseph Smith the Prophet, and his Progenitors for many Generations* (London: S. W. Richards, 1853 [reprint London: William Bowden, 1969]), 53.
6. Lucy Mack Smith, *History of Joseph Smith by His Mother* ed. Preston Nibley (Salt Lake City: Bookcraft, 1958), 46, 51.
7. Smith, *Biographical Sketches*, 62–63.

8.   Joseph Smith, "Manuscript History of the Church," Book
        A-1, 131, Church History Library, The Church of Jesus
        Christ of Latter-day Saints, Salt Lake City.

9.   Smith, *Biographical Sketches,* 65.

10.   Smith, "Manuscript History of the Church," Book A-1,
        131.

11.   Smith, *Biographical Sketches,* 67-68.

12.   Smith, *Biographical Sketches,* 70.

13.   Smith, "Manuscript History of the Church," Book A-1,
        131–32.

14.   Smith, *Biographical Sketches,* 71.

15.   J. W. Peterson, "William Smith Interview," *Deseret Evening
        News* 28, no. 11 (January 20, 1894): 11.

16.   Smith, *Biographical Sketches,* 72–73.

17.   Peterson, "William Smith Interview," 11.

18.   Smith, *Biographical Sketches,* 73.

19.   See Joseph Smith—History 1:21.

20.   Joseph Smith—History 1:15–17. For a full account see
        Joseph Smith—History 1:11-20.

21.   Joseph Smith—History 1:21–22.

22.   Eber D. Howe, *Mormonism Unvailed: or, A Faithful
        Account of that Singular Imposition and Delusion, from its
        Rise to the Present Time. With Sketches of the Characters
        of Its Propagators, and a Full Detail of the Manner in
        which the Famous Golden Bible was Brought Before the
        World. To which are Added, Inquiries into the Probability
        that the Historical Part of the Said Bible was Written by
        One Solomon Spalding, More than Twenty Years Ago, and
        by Him Intended to Have Been Published as a Romance*
        (Painesville, Ohio: E. B. Howe, 1834), 248–61.

23.   Peterson, "William Smith, Interview," 11.

24.   Joseph Smith—History 1:28.

25.   Joseph Smith Jr., "Brother O. Cowdery," *Latter-day Saints'
        Messenger and Advocate* 1, no. 3 (December 1834): 40.

26.   Joseph Smith—History 1:27, 29.

27.   Joseph Smith—History 1:29–30, 33.

28.   Joseph Smith—History 1:33, 35, 42, 51, 53.

29.   Smith, *Biographical Sketches,* 103.

30. Andrew Jensen, *Journal History of the Church of Jesus Christ of Latter-day Saints, 1830-1972* (Salt Lake City: Church of Jesus Christ of Latter-day Saints, 1906 [January 20, 1894]), Church History Library.

31. "Autobiography of Wandle Mace," typescript, 47. L. Tom Perry Special Collections, Harold B. Lee Library, Brigham Young University, Provo, Utah.

32. Smith, *Biographical Sketches*, 103.

33. Joseph Smith—History 1:56.

34. Joseph Smith—History 1:57.

35. Smith, *History of the Church*, 1:17.

36. Statement of Isaac Hale, reprinted in Emily C. Blackman, *History of Susquehanna County, Pennsylvania* (Philadelphia, Pennsylvania: Claxton, Remsen, and Haffelfinger, 1873), 578.

37. Smith, *Biographical Sketches*, 105.

38. Joseph Smith III, "Last Testimony of Sister Emma," *Saints' Herald* 26, no. 19 (October 1, 1879): 289–90. Emma Smith Bidamon gave this testimony in an interview, February 4–10, 1879 with her son Joseph Smith III.

39. Joseph Smith—History 1:59.

40. Smith, *History of the Church*, 6:74.

41. Joseph Smith III, "Last Testimony of Sister Emma," *Saints' Herald* 26, no. 19 (October 1, 1879): 289–90.

42. Journal of Reuben Miller, October 21, 1848. See also Richard L. Anderson, "Reuben Miller, Recorder of Oliver Cowdery's Reaffirmations," *BYU Studies* 8, no. 3 (Spring 1968): 277–93.

43. Smith, *History of the Church*, 1:39–41; Doctrine and Covenants 13.

44. Joseph Smith—History 1:68–70, 72. Italics in original.

45. See Doctrine and Covenants 27:12.

46. Preston Nibley, *Witnesses of the Book of Mormon* (Salt Lake City: Stevens and Wallis, 1946), 48–49.

47. "The Testimony of the Three Witnesses," *The Book of Mormon* (New York: Simon and Schuster, 1993).

48. Smith, *History of the Church*, 4:461.

49. Smith, *History of the Church*, 1:78.

50. Doctrine and Covenants 21:1.

51. Smith, *History of the Church*, 5:498.

52. Wilford Woodruff, in *Official Report of the Annual General Conference of the Church of Jesus Christ of Latter-day Saints* (Salt Lake City: The Church of Jesus Christ of Latter-day Saints, 1830–2007), April 1898, 57.

53. Doctrine and Covenants 37:1.

54. *History of Geauga and Lake Counties, Ohio*, 248, as cited in Milton V. Backman Jr., *The Heavens Resound, A History of the Latter-day Saints in Ohio, 1830–1838* (Salt Lake City: Deseret Book, 1983), 47.

55. Oliver Cowdery, quoted in W. A. Cowdery, ed., "The Change of Times...,"*Latter-day Saints' Messenger and Advocate* 3, no. 9 (June 1837): 520.

56. Smith, *History of the Church*, 1:261–64, 450.

57. Smith, *History of the Church*, 1:245; 6:50.

58. Doctrine and Covenants 76:22–23.

59. Smith, *History of the Church*, 5:362.

60. Smith, *History of the Church*, 1:454; 2:73, 114.

61. Smith, *History of the Church*, 2:144.

62. Doctrine and Covenants 88:119.

63. Smith, *Biographical Sketches*, 248.

64. Smith, *History of the Church*, 1:349.

65. Smith, *Biographical Sketches*, 249.

66. Orson F. Whitney, *Life of Heber C. Kimball, an Apostle, the Father and Founder of the British Mission* (Salt Lake City: Juvenile Instructor Office, 1888), 46.

67. Smith, *Biographical Sketches*, 249.

68. "Autobiography of Benjamin Brown (1794–1853)," *Testimonies for the Truth* (Liverpool: S. W. Richards, 1853), 6.

69. *Hymns of the Church of Jesus Christ of Latter-day Saints* (Salt Lake City: The Church of Jesus Christ of Latter-day Saints, 1985), 2.

70. Smith, *History of the Church*, 2:428.

71. Doctrine and Covenants 110: Introduction, 1–3, 7, 10.

72. Benjamin F. Johnson, *My Life's Review: Autobiography of Benjamin F. Johnson* (Provo, Utah: Grandin Book, 1997), 28–29.

73.   Smith, *History of the Church*, 2:487.

74.   Smith, *Biographical Sketches*, 266.

75.   Smith, *Biographical Sketches*, 267.

76.   Journal of John Smith, April 23, 1838. Church History Library.

77.   Smith, *History of the Church*, 3:2–3, 8–9, 225.

78.   Smith, *History of the Church*, 1:391. See also "Autobiography of Edward Partridge," July 20, 1833, Church History Library.

79.   "Autobiography of Levi Ward Hancock," typescript, 50. Church History Library.

80.   "Newell Knight's Journal," *Classic Experiences and Adventures* (Salt Lake City: Bookcraft, 1969), 97.

81.   Correspondence from Governor Lilburn W. Boggs to Headquarters Militia, City of Jefferson, October 27, 1838, as cited in Smith, *History of the Church*, 3:175. Italics in original.

82.   Smith, *History of the Church*, 3:420.

83.   Smith, *History of the Church*, 4:370.

84.   Titus Billings, "Titus Billings," *Mormon Redress Petitions: Documents of the 1833–1838 Missouri Conflict* ed. Clark V. Johnson (Provo, Utah: Religious Studies Center, Brigham Young University, 1992), 140.

85.   Parley P. Pratt, *Autobiography of Parley P. Pratt, One of the Twelve Apostles of the Church of Jesus Christ of Latter-day Saints, Embracing His Life, Ministry, and Travels, With Extracts, In Prose and Verse, From His Miscellaneous Writings* ed. Parley P. Pratt (Salt Lake City: Deseret Book, 1950 [Revised and enhanced by Scot Facer Proctor and Maurine Jensen Proctor, 2000]), 234–35.

86.   Pratt, *Autobiography*, 236.

87.   Pratt, *Autobiography*, 239. Italics in original.

88.   Smith, *History of the Church*, 3:200–1.

89.   Pratt, *Autobiography*, 240.

90.   Pratt, *Autobiography*, 244.

91.   Smith, *History of the Church*, 3:226–29.

92.   Smith, *History of the Church*, 4:540. See also *Times and Seasons* 3, no. 9 (March 1, 1842): 709.

93.   Letter from Joseph Smith to Emma Smith, November 12, 1838, as cited in Dean C. Jessee, *The Personal Writings of Joseph Smith* (Salt Lake City: Deseret Book, 1984), 368.

94.   Pratt, *Autobiography*, 262–63. Italics in original.

95.   E. Robinson, "Items of Personal History," *The Return*, 2 (March 1890), as cited in Stephen C. LeSueur, *The 1838 Mormon War in Missouri* (Columbia, Missouri: University of Missouri Press, 1987), 198.

96.   Pratt, *Autobiography*, 272–74.

97.   Pratt, *Autobiography*, 276. Italics in original.

98.   Letter from Joseph Smith to the Church in Caldwell County, December 16, 1838, Liberty, Missouri, as quoted in Jessee, *Personal Writings of Joseph Smith*, 377.

99.   Letter from Joseph Smith to Emma Smith, April 4, 1839, Liberty, Missouri, quoted in Jessee, *Personal Writings of the Prophet Joseph Smith*, 408.

100.   Letter from Joseph Smith to Emma Smith, March 21, 1839, Liberty, Missouri, quoted in Jessee, *Personal Writings of the Prophet Joseph Smith*, 426.

101.   Doctrine and Covenants 121:33.

102.   Doctrine and Covenants 121:1–2, 7–10; 122:7–9.

103.   Smith, *History of the Church*, 3:320, 423.

104.   Pratt, *Autobiography*, 354.

105.   Smith, *History of the Church*, 4:165–66.

106.   Smith, *History of the Church*, 4:80. Italics in original.

107.   Smith, *History of the Church*, 3:375.

108.   Smith, *Biographical Sketches*, 338.

109.   Matthias Cowley, *Wilford Woodruff, History of His Life and Labors* (Salt Lake City: Bookcraft, 1964), 104.

110.   W. W. Phelps made this statement to Emma Smith. Smith, *History of the Church*, 6:33, 165–66.

111.   Cowley, *Wilford Woodruff, History of His Life and Labors*, 105.

112.   Smith, *History of the Church*, 5:232.

113.   "Harvey Cluff Autobiography," typescript, 4–5. Perry Special Collections.

114.   J. H. Buckingham, quoted in Stanley B. Kimball, "Nauvoo," *The Improvement Era* 65, no. 7 (July 1962): 548.

115. George A. Smith, "Historical Address by President George A. Smith," October 8–9 1868, as reported by David W. Evans, *Journal of Discourses* 26 vols. (Liverpool: Latter Day Saints' Book Depot, 1854-1886), 13:115.

116. E. Cecil McGavin, *Nauvoo, the Beautiful* (Salt Lake City: Bookcraft, 1972), 85–86.

117. J. Earl Arrington, "William Weeks, Architect of the Nauvoo Temple," *BYU Studies* 9, no. 3 (Spring 1979): 341, 346.

118. "Wandle Mace Autobiography," typescript, 94, Perry Special Collections.

119. Smith, *History of the Church*, 6:58.

120. *Warsaw Signal*, May 29, 1844.

121. Smith, *History of the Church*, 3:368–69.

122. Smith, *History of the Church*, 2:437.

123. Mercy Thompson, "Recollections of the Prophet Joseph Smith," *Juvenile Instructor* 27, no. 13 (July 1, 1892): 399.

124. Smith, *History of the Church*, 5:166–67.

125. Smith, *History of the Church*, 5:252.

126. Jesse Crosby, quoted in Hyrum L. Andrus and Helen Mae Andrus, *They Knew the Prophet* (Salt Lake City: Bookcraft, 1974 [reprint, Deseret Book, 1999]), 145.

127. Smith, *History of the Church*, 5:401.

128. Smith, *History of the Church*, 6:151–52.

129. Smith, *History of the Church*, 6:152. Italics in original.

130. Smith, *History of Joseph Smith by His Mother*, 322.

131. Quoted in Roger D. Launius, "Anti-Mormonism in Illinois: Thomas C. Sharp's Unfinished History of the Mormon War, 1845," *Journal of Mormon History* 15 (1989): 30.

132. *Warsaw Signal*, May 29, 1844.

133. Smith, *History of the Church*, 6:499.

134. Smith, *History of the Church*, 6:545.

135. Smith, *History of the Church*, 6:549, 555. Italics in original.

136. Smith, *History of the Church*, 6:566. Italics in original.

137. B. H. Roberts, *A Comprehensive History of the Church of Jesus Christ of Latter-day Saints* 6 vols. (Provo, Utah: Brigham Young University Press, 1965), 2:281.

138. Smith, *History of the Church*, 6:605.

139. Smith, *History of the Church*, 6: 615.

140. Doctrine and Covenants 135:1.

141. Doctrine and Covenants 135:1. Italics in original.

142. Smith, *History of the Church*, 6: 618.

143. Doctrine and Covenants 135:1. Italics in original.

144. Doctrine and Covenants 135:7.

145. Ronald K. Esplin, "Life in Nauvoo, June 1844: Vilate Kimball's Martyrdom Letters," *BYU Studies* 19, no. 2 (Winter 1979): 238.

146. Smith, *History of the Church*, 7:156.

147. Smith, *History of the Church*, 7:106.

148. William G. Hartley, *"They are My Friends," A History of the Joseph Knight Family, 1825–1850* (Provo, Utah: Grandin Book Company, 1986), 153–54. See also William G. Hartley, *Stand by My Servant Joseph: The Story of the Joseph Knight Family and the Restoration* (Provo, Utah: Joseph Fielding Smith Institute for Latter-day Saint History, Brigham Young University, and Salt Lake City: Deseret Book, 2003).

149. *New York Herald*, July 8, 1844.

150. Smith, *History of the Church*, 7:198.

151. Smith, *History of the Church*, 3:30. See also *Elders' Journal*, July 1838, 44.

152. See Articles of Faith 1:1–13. Smith, *History of the Church*, 4: 535–41. Italics in original.

153. Smith, *History of the Church*, 6:50. See also *Times and Seasons* 4, no. 21 (September 15, 1843): 331–32.

154. Smith, *History of the Church*, 1:188–89.

155. Smith, *History of the Church*, 2:11, 14. See also "The Elders of the Church in Kirtland, to Their Brethren Abroad," *Evening and Morning Star* 2, no. 17 (February 1834): 136.

156. Smith, *History of the Church*, 5:31. See also Joseph Smith, "Gift of the Holy Ghost," *Times and Seasons* 3, no. 16 (June 15, 1842): 825.

157. Smith, *History of the Church*, 5:498–99.

158. Smith, *History of the Church*, 3:303–4.

159. Smith, *History of the Church*, 4:492–93.

160. Smith, *History of the Church*, 5:426.

161. Smith, *History of the Church*, 6:303–5.

162. Joseph Smith, Discourse, July 23, 1843, Joseph Smith Collection Addresses, Church History Library.

163. From Joseph Smith to the editor of the *Chester County Register and Examiner*, January 25, 1840, Brandywine, Pennsylvania.

164. Smith, *History of the Church*, 4:358.

165. Letter from Joseph Smith and high priests to brethren at Geneseo, New York, November 23, 1833, Church History Library.

166. Smith, *History of the Church*, 5:27. See also Joseph Smith, "Gift of the Holy Ghost," *Times and Seasons* 3, no. 16 (June 15, 1842): 823.

167. James Burgess Journals, 1841–48, vol. 2. Church History Library.

168. Smith, *History of the Church*, 4:555.

169. *Lectures on Faith* (American Fork: Covenant, 2000), 3–5.

170. *Lectures on Faith*, 74–75.

171. Smith, *History of the Church*, 1:316.

172. Smith, *History of the Church*, 3:379.

173. Smith, *History of the Church*, 4:553–54.

174. Smith, *History of the Church*, 4:554–55.

175. Joseph Smith, "Baptism," *Times and Seasons* 3, no. 9 (September 1, 1842): 903–5.

176. Smith, *History of the Church*, 4:554.

177. Smith, *History of the Church*, 4:555.

178. "Letter from Joseph Smith to Isaac Galland, March 22, 1839, Liberty Jail," *Times and Seasons* 1, no. 4 (February 1840): 54.

179. Smith, *History of the Church*, 5:499.

180. Smith, *History of the Church*, 5:31. See also Joseph Smith, "Gift of the Holy Ghost," *Times and Seasons* 3, no. 16 (June 15, 1842): 825.

181. Joseph Smith, "To the Saints of God," *Times and Seasons* 3, no. 24 (October 15, 1842): 952.

182. Smith, *History of the Church*, 3:295–96.

183.   Smith, *History of the Church*, 6:306–7.
184.   Smith, *History of the Church*, 3:381.
185.   Smith, *History of the Church*, 4:571.
186.   "Letter from Joseph Smith to Isaac Galland, March 22, 1839, Liberty Jail," *Times and Seasons* 1, no. 4 (February 1840): 54.
187.   Smith, *History of the Church*, 3:385–87.
188.   Doctrine and Covenants 107:1–5, 8, 18–19.
189.   Smith, *History of the Church*, 4:555.
190.   Smith, *History of the Church*, 2:14. Italics in original. See also "The Elders of the Church in Kirtland, to Their Brethren Abroad," *Evening and Morning Star* 2, no. 18 (March 1834):142.
191.   Smith, *History of the Church*, 4:554.
192.   Smith, *History of the Church*, 4:45. See also "Letter from Joseph Smith and his Counselors in the First Presidency to the Saints, November 1839, Commerce, Illinois," *Times and Seasons* 1, no. 2 (December 1839): 29.
193.   Smith, *History of the Church*, 4:45.
194.   William Clayton, book. Church History Library.
195.   Smith, *History of the Church*, 4:574. See also Joseph Smith, "Try the Saints," *Times and Seasons* 3, no. 11 (April 1, 1842): 744.
196.   Letter from Joseph Smith to Thomas Ford, June 22, 1844, Nauvoo. Joseph Smith, Collection. Church History Library
197.   Smith, *History of the Church*, 5:424.
198.   Smith, *History of the Church*, 6:184.
199.   Smith, *History of the Church*, 6:312–13.
200.   Smith, *History of the Church*, 6:139.
201.   Smith, *History of the Church*, 5:362.
202.   Smith, *History of the Church*, 6:365; 5:425–26.
203.   Smith, *History of the Church*, 4:553–54.
204.   Smith, *History of the Church*, 5:361–63.
205.   Smith, *History of the Church*, 6:315–16.
206.   Smith, *History of the Church*, 4:227.
207.   Smith, *History of the Church*, 5:517.

208.   Smith, *History of the Church*, 2:229, fn. See also "To the
        Saints Scattered Abroad," *Messenger and Advocate* 1, no. 9
        (June 1835): 137.

209.   Joseph Smith, "To the Saints of God," *Times and Seasons*
        3, no. 24 (October 15, 1842): 952.

210.   Smith, *History of the Church*, 4:606.

211.   Joseph Smith, "On the Duty of Husband and Wife,"
        Elders' Journal 1, no. 4 (August 1838): 61.

212.   Joseph Smith, "On the Duty of Husband and Wife,"
        Elders' Journal 1, no. 4 (August 1838): 61.

213.   Smith, *History of the Church*, 4:605–7.

214.   Smith, *History of the Church*, 2:342.

215.   Smith, *History of the Church*, 4:337. See also "Report from
        Joseph Smith and his Counselors in the First Presidency,
        April 7, 1841," *Times and Seasons* 2, no. 12 (April 15,
        1841): 385.

216.   Smith, *History of the Church*, 2:353.

217.   Smith, *History of the Church*, 3:390.

218.   Smith, *History of the Church*, 5:337.

219.   Thomas Cottam (1820–1896), high priest; endowed
        in Nauvoo Temple. Thomas Cottam, quoted in
        "Recollections of the Prophet Joseph Smith," *Juvenile
        Instructor* 27, no. 2 (January 15, 1892): 65.

220.   Daniel Duncan McArthur (1820–1903), high priest;
        bishop; endowed in Nauvoo Temple. Daniel McArthur,
        quoted in "Recollections of the Prophet Joseph Smith,"
        Juvenile Instructor 27 no. 4 (February 15, 1892): 129.

221.   Brigham Young (1801–1877), 2nd President of the Church
        of Jesus Christ of Latter-day Saints. Brigham Young,
        "Faith, etc.," *Journal of Discourses* 26 vols. (Liverpool: F. D.
        and S. W. Richards, 1854-1886), 3:51.

222.   Wilford Woodruff (1807–1898), 4th President of the Church
        of Jesus Christ of Latter-day Saints. Wilford Woodruff,
        Deseret News: Semi-Weekly, November 25, 1873, 1.

223.   Mosiah Lyman Hancock (1834–1909), seventy; endowed
        in Nauvoo Temple; mission to Moquis Indians. "Mosiah
        L. Hancock Autobiography," typescript, 22, Church
        History Library.

224. Mercy Rachel Fielding Thompson (1807–1893), endowed in Nauvoo Temple; member of Female Relief Society of Nauvoo. Mercy Thompson, quoted in "Recollections of the Prophet Joseph Smith," *Juvenile Instructor* 27, no. 13 (July 1, 1892): 399.

225. Mary Alice Cannon Lambert (1828–1920), endowed in Nauvoo Temple. Mary Lambert, quoted in "Joseph Smith, the Prophet," *Young Woman's Journal* 16, no. 12 (December 1905): 554.

226. Parley Parker Pratt (1807–1857), apostle. Pratt, *Autobiography*, 259-60.

227. John Needham (1819–1901), seventy; missionary to Wales. "Letter from John Needham to Thomas Ward, July 7, 1843, Nauvoo, Illinois," *Millennial Star* 4, no. 6 (October 1843): 89.

228. William Clayton (1814–1879), high priest; endowed in Nauvoo Temple. missionary to England. Letter from William Clayton to Edward Martin, December 10, 1840, Nauvoo, Illinois, Church History Library.

229. Alvah Jedethan Alexander (1831–1917), Sunday school superintendent; bishop's counselor. Alvah Alexander, quoted in "Joseph Smith, the Prophet," *Young Woman's Journal* 17, no. 12 (December 1906): 541.

230. Pratt, *Autobiography*, 32.

231. Wilford Woodruff, *Deseret News: Semi-Weekly*, October 18, 1881, 1.

232. Wandle Mace (1809–1890), high priest; endowed in Nauvoo Temple; mission to New York. "Wandle Mace Autobiography," typescript, 102, Church History Library.

233. Orson Spencer (1802–1855), high priest; endowed in Nauvoo Temple; mission to Connecticut. Orson Spencer, "Letter of Orson Spencer, November 17, 1842, Nauvoo, Illinois," *Times and Seasons* 14, no. 4 (January 2, 1843): 56-57.

234. Brigham Young, *Deseret News*, August 27, 1862, 65.

235. Edwin Holden (1807–1894), endowed in Nauvoo Temple. Edwin Holden, quoted in "Recollections of the Prophet Joseph Smith," *Juvenile Instructor* 27, no. 5 (March 1, 1892): 153.

236. John Taylor (1808–1887), 3rd President of the Church of Jesus Christ of Latter-day Saints. John Taylor, "The Organization of the Church," *Millennial Star* 13, no. 22 (November 15, 1851): 339.

237. Wilford Woodruff, *Deseret Weekly*, December 25, 1897, 34.

238. Franklin Dewey Richards (1821–1899), apostle. Franklin D. Richards, "A Tour of Historical Scenes," *The Contributor* 7, no. 8 (May 1886): 301.

239. Mary Elizabeth Rollins Lightner (1818–1917), endowed in Nauvoo Temple. Remarks by Mary E. Lightner, April 14, 1905, Brigham Young University, 1. Perry Special Collections.

240. Joseph Lee Robinson (1811–1893), high priest; endowed in the Nauvoo Temple; counselor to bishop. Joseph Robinson, quoted in Andrus and Andrus, *They Knew the Prophet*, 64.

241. Andrew Jackson Workman (1824–1909), seventy; endowed in Nauvoo Temple; missionary in South Carolina. Andrew Workman, quoted in "Recollections of the Prophet Joseph Smith," *Juvenile Instructor* 27, no. 20 (October 15, 1892): 641.

242. "Wandle Mace Autobiography," typescript, 102–3.

243. Wilford Woodruff Journals, 1833–1898, entry February 19, 1842.

244. Brigham Young, "Intelligence, etc.," *Journal of Discourses*, 7:289–90.

245. William Henrie (1799–1883), high priest; endowed in Nauvoo Temple. William Henrie, quoted in Morley, "History of William and Myra Mayall Henrie," 4.

246. John Taylor, quoted in Smith, *History of the Church*, 7:106.

247.   Pratt, *Autobiography*, 260–61.

248.   John Lyman Smith (1828–1898), seventy; endowed in
       Nauvoo Temple; president of Swiss and Italian Mission.
       "John Lyman Smith Autobiography and Diaries, 1846-
       1895," entry of September 1839, Church History Library.

249.   Lorenzo Snow (1814–1901), 5th President of the Church of
       Jesus Christ of Latter-day Saints. Lorenzo Snow, *Deseret
       Weekly*, April 13, 1889, 387.

250.   Howard Coray (1817–1908), high priest; clerk for Joseph
       Smith; endowed in Nauvoo Temple; served missions to
       Pennsylvania and Southern States. Letter from Howard
       Coray to Martha Jane Lewis, August 2, 1889, Church
       History Library.

251.   George Washington Taggart (1816–1893), high priest;
       endowed in Nauvoo Temple; Mormon Battalion. George
       Taggart, quoted in Ronald O. Barney, "'A Man That You
       Could Not Help Likeing,' Joseph Smith and Nauvoo
       Portrayed in a Letter by Susannah and George Taggart,"
       BYU Studies 40, no. 2 (2001):172–73.

252.   Jane Snyder Richards (1823-1912) member of Female
       Relief Society of Nauvoo; Utah representative to National
       Council of Women in 1891. Jane Richards, quoted in
       "Joseph Smith, the Prophet," *Young Woman's Journal* 16,
       no 12 (December 1905): 550.

253.   George Albert Smith (1817–1875), First Quorum of the
       Seventy; apostle. George A. Smith, "Memoirs of George A.
       Smith," n.p., n.d., 36. Perry Special Collections.

254.   Henry William Bigler (1815–1900), Mormon Battalion;
       mission president in Sandwich Islands; temple worker.
       Henry Bigler, quoted in "Recollections of the Prophet
       Joseph Smith," *Juvenile Instructor* 2, no. 5 (March 1,
       1892): 151–52.

255.   William Harrison Maughan (1834–1905), high priest;
       bishop; patriarch. William Harrison Maughan Family
       History (Providence, Utah: Keith W. Watkins & Sons,
       Inc., 1986), 6.

256. William Carter Staines (1818–1881), endowed in Nauvoo
Temple; emigration agent for the Church. "Reminiscences
of William C. Staines," *The Contributor* 12, no. 4
(February 1891): 122.

257. John Milton Bernhisel (1799–1881), high priest; bishop;
Utah delegate to Congress. Smith, *History of the Church*,
6:468.

258. Jesse Nathaniel Smith (1834–1906), high priest; mayor;
member of stake presidency. Jesse Smith, quoted in
"Recollections of the Prophet Joseph Smith," *Juvenile
Instructor* 27, no. 2 (January 15, 1892): 23–24.

259. Roberts, *Comprehensive History*, 2:349–50.

260. William W. Phelps, "Praise to the Man," *Hymns*, no. 27,
verses 1–2.

261. Smith, *History of Joseph Smith by His Mother*, 222.

262. Brian H. Stuy, ed., *Collected Discourses Delivered by
Wilford Woodruff, His Two Counselors, the Twelve
Apostles, and Others*, 5 vols. (Burbank, California: B.H.S.
Publishing, 1987–1992), 5:317–18.

Author Biographical Information

Susan Easton Black is a professor of Church History and Doctrine at Brigham Young University. She is a former Associate Dean of General Education and Honors and an Eliza R. Snow fellow. Professor Black is the recipient of many academic awards, including the Karl G. Maeser Distinguished Faculty Lecturer Award, the first female faculty member at BYU to be so honored. She has written over 100 books and 250 articles.